EXCEL VBA &

EXCEL PIVOT

TABLES CRASH COURSE

Ultimate Crash Course to Learn It Well and Become an Expert in VBA,Excel Macros & Pivot Tables.

Smarter Way to Learn it faster and Remember it longer

TABLE OF CONTENTS

EXCEL VBA
A STEP-BY-STEP GUIDE TO LEARN
AND MASTER EXCEL VBA PROGRAMMING

EXCEL VBA
TOP TIPS, TRICKS, TIMESAVERS, AND COMMON MISTAKES IN VBA PROGRAMMING

EXCEL MACROS
A STEP-BY-STEP GUIDE TO LEARN AND MASTER EXCEL MACROS

EXCEL PIVOTTABLES AND DASHBOARD
THE STEP-BY-STEP GUIDE TO LEARN AND MASTER EXCEL
PIVOTTABLES AND DASHBOARD

Excel VBA

A Step-By-Step Guide To Learn And Master Excel VBA Programming

Part One:
For Beginning Programmers

Introduction

I want to thank you and congratulate you for purchasing the book *Excel VBA: A Step-By-Step Guide To Learn And Master Excel VBA Programming*. Now, you are one step closer to understanding how to use VBA Programing to make using Excel a piece of cake.

Excel VBA, or what coders might refer to as Visual Basic for Applications, is a built-in coding program found in Microsoft Office's Excel. This program is all about turning repetitive or complicated tasks into applications that Excel will run for you behind the scenes. By following the steps in this book, you will be able to create applications customized for your needs. In turn, these applications will help you use Excel more effectively and efficiently. You'll be able to accomplish what you do now in Excel in half the time!

And don't panic. This book was written with beginners in mind. So, no background in coding is required. Just follow the steps outlined in the book in order to accomplish the task you want, and you should see fast results. Also, keep in mind that the instructions provided in this book have been written using the Excel 2016 layout. If you are using a later version of Excel, these instructions will still work, but note that you might have to find the button or tab in a different location.

In total, this book contains fifteen chapters that each covers a basic function of Excel VBA. Many of these functions build off of each other. So, if you are new to VBA coding, it's important that you start at the beginning and work your way through each chapter. Otherwise, some of the language or steps might be confusing. At the beginning of each chapter, you will find a list of definitions for the major terms that will be used throughout that chapter. Each chapter will also contain a step-by-step process for creating and running the function covered in the chapter as well as a way to practice the skill you just learned.

Thanks again for purchasing this book. I hope it will help you understand Excel VBA and help you accomplish your goals.

Chapter 1

VBA Overview

The acronym VBA stands for Visual Basic for Applications, and it is a hidden gem found in Excel. Using this function of Excel, you will be able to create applications customized for to your needs such as automatically analyzing a chart of data, using formulas to collect data, or creating dialogue boxes and customized user forms. Using Excel VBA does not require that you install any additional software. Instead, all you need is the basic Excel program available from Microsoft Office. The instructions in this book use Excel 2016 as the example, but you can perform all of these same functions with later versions of Excel.

As you progress through each chapter of this book, there are a few terms that you might find unfamiliar. Here, we've provided you with a short list of basic terminologies that you can refer to throughout your study of this chapter.

Macros: a program set of commands that run Excel functions automatically.

Dialogue Box: a sub-menu or small window that requires further action from the user to operate.

Before we can dive in to creating these amazing programs, we need to add the Developer Toolbar to Excel. This toolbar contains all the buttons that you will need to be a successful VBA Programmer. To add this toolbar, just follow the steps below:

How to display the "Developer" tab:

1- Open Microsoft Office Excel.

2- Click on the "File" tab, the first tab that currently appears on your toolbar.

3- Now click on "Options." In Excel 2016, the "Options" button appears at the very bottom of the list.

4- After clicking on this tab, a dialog box will open that contains a lot of information. Right now, keep your attention focused on the left-hand column that contains a list of more tabs. Find the tab that says, "Customize Ribbon." Click that tab.

5- After clicking on this tab, the dialogue box will change to show you two columns. The one on the left says, "Choose commands from" and contains a menu with all the popular commands. The column on the right says, "Customize the Ribbon" and shows a menu that lists all the current tabs on your toolbar. In this menu, find the box next to "Developer," it's near the bottom of the menu and check box.

6- Exit out of the dialogue box.

7- Look at your current toolbar now. It should contain the "Developer" tab near the end. It looks something like this:

With this tab installed, you are now ready to begin VBA programming!

Another task you might want to perform before beginning the lessons found in the other chapters is removing the security warning. This will allow you to run customized applications without having to go through the tedious process of accepting each application one-by-one. With the security warning disabled, you will be able to run all the applications you want without any warnings popping up. If you are not using a personal computer to run these applications, you might want to keep the security warning up. The security warning might also be helpful if you want the opportunity to double check the application before it runs each time. It's up to you to choose. But if you want to disable the security warning, simply follow the steps below:

How To Disable Security Warnings:

1- Click on the "Macro Security" button on your "Developer" tab. You can see it in the image above. It has the icon of a yellow triangle with an exclamation mark inside it.

2- Once you click on this button, it will bring up a dialogue box called "Trust" that opens automatically to "Macro Settings."

3- In the main part of the dialogue box, you will see a menu that has two parts: "Macro Settings" and "Developer Macro Settings." Focus your attention to the part that says, "Developer Macro Settings."

4- Under this heading, you will see a box with the words "Trust access to the VBA project object model." By clicking this box, you will be allowing any application that you create through the VBA programmer to run automatically without a security warning. Click on this box if you want to disable the security warnings.

Now that you have found out where the "Developer" tab is located and decided how you want to handle security warnings, it's time to start programing!

Chapter 2

VBA Programming Variables

Now that you have the basics under your belt, you are ready to try your hand at programming. We're going to start out by defining some variables. Then we will set up a program that can add, subtract, multiply and divide these variables.

When setting up a variable, there are a few options to choose from:

Integer: If you are working with whole numbers, you will most likely use this variable type. However, this variable can only store numbers from -32,768 to +32,767. If you need to work with a larger number, use the variable type Long.

Long: This variable also indicates whole numbers, but those that fall outside the range of the variable Integer.

String: If you are working with text or other characters that are not numbers, you will use this variable.

Single: Use this variable type if you are working with fractions or decimals. It will hold up to 4 bytes of data.

Double: Like the Single variable, this variable also works with fractions or decimals. However, it can hold up to 8 bytes of data, so it can be used with more precision.

To begin setting up a variable, you will need to open the Visual Basic Editor. You open this by clicking on the "Visual Basic" button on the "Developer" tab. In Excel 2016, the "Visual Basic" button is the very first button on the left. Clicking on this button will open up a separate window that looks something like this:

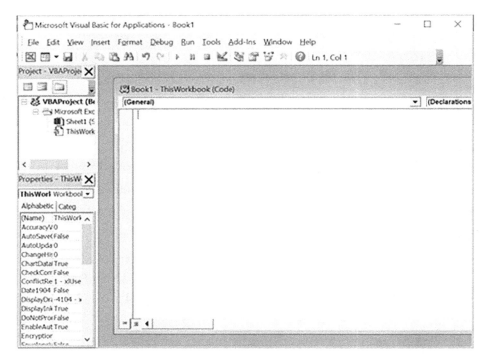

This is the window in which you will write all the programming. Let's start by setting up a simple variable.

How to set up a Variable:

1- Begin by typing "Sub" and then type "PracticeVariable." This is the title that we are going to give this set of instructions.

2- Press the "Enter" key. This will automatically set the "Sub" and "End Sub" for your first program.

3- Next type "Dim," space, "FirstNumber," "As Integer." This sets up your variable name as "FirstNumber" and defines its value as an integer.

4- Press enter and type "FirstNumber=10." Now we've defined the value of this variable as "10."

5- Now that we've set up the variable's value, let's define the variable's range. Press enter again and type a new line. First, you want to define what worksheet you want your variable to appear. Let's select Worksheet 1. Write "Worksheets(1)." Make sure "Worksheets" is plural in your code. If not, you will receive an error message.

6- In this same line of code, we are now going to define what cell we want the variable to appear in. Let's select cell A1. Write "Range("A1")." This indicates that your variable will appear in the cell A1.

7- Now. we want to indicate what variable will appear here. In the same line of code, write "Value=FirstNumber"; your entire line of code should look like this: Worksheets(1).Range("A1").Value=FirstNumber

8- After typing out the program, your code should look like this:

```
Book1 - ThisWorkbook (Code)

(General)

Sub Variable_Practice()
Dim FirstNumber As Integer
FirstNumber = 10
Worksheets(1).Range("A1").Value = FirstNumber

End Sub
```

9- Now that we've set up the program, we're ready to run it. In the Visual Basic Editor's main menu, there is a tab that says "Run." You can see this tab in the first image of the chapter. Click on this tab and then click on the first option in the pull down menu, "Run Sub/User Form." Or you can click on the small, green sideways triangle. That will also run the application.

10- Switch back over to your Excel Sheet by pressing the Excel icon, the first button in your Visual Basic Editor tool bar. You should see that the number 10 has appeared in cell A1.

Congratulations! You just ran your very first customized program! Now, let's make it a bit more complicated by creating a program that can add, subtract, multiply, or divide numbers for us.

How to set up a program that runs mathematical functions:

1- Open up the Visual Basic Editor and create a new code. You can continue to type the code in the same window. After "End Sub," begin typing "Sub" and add "Addition" for its name.

2- Because we are going to be running mathematical functions, we will need more than one variable. We are going to begin by defining the value of each variable. First type "Dim FirstNumber As Integer". Press enter and repeat this process for another variable called SecondNumber.

3- Next. define the numerical value of both variables. In the example code, I chose to define FirstNumber as 10 and SecondNumber as 25. You can choose any integer value you want. So far, your code should look like this:

Sub Addition()

Dim FirstNumber As Integer

Dim SecondNumber As Integer

FirstNumber = 10

SecondNumber = 25

4- Now that we've set up the values of each variable, we are ready to write the program that adds these variables together. We are also going to write a code so that one of the cells contains the word "Answers" and another cell contains the answer to 10+25.

5- In a new line, type "Worksheets(1).Range("A1").Value= "Answer". This will allow the word "Answer" to appear in cell A1.

6- Press enter and write a new line of text. It should read Worksheets(1).Range("B1").Value=FirstNumber+SecondNumber

7- Now that we've created the program, we are ready to run it. Either click on the side-ways green arrow or the "Run" tab.

8- Go back to your Excel spreadsheet. You should see the word "Answer" in cell A1 and the number 35 in cell B1.

Congratulations! You just ran a program that performed a simple mathematical function. You can easily modify this code to perform other mathematical functions, such as subtraction, multiplication or division. For example, below is a program similar to the one we just wrote that multiplies instead of adding:

Sub Multiplication()

Dim FirstNumber As Integer

Dim SecondNumber As Integer

FirstNumber=10

SecondNumber=25

Worksheets(1).Range("A1").Value= "Answer"

Worksheets(1).Range("B1").Value=FirstNumber*SecondNumber

Recognize that depending on what mathematical function you want to run, you will use a different symbol. The addition requires the plus sign (+), subtraction uses the minus sign (-), multiplication uses the asterisk (*), and division requires the forward slash (/).

Before moving on to the next chapter, practice writing a few different programs that perform different mathematical functions. After you've mastered the codes needed to create these programs, you will be ready to move onto the next skill.

Chapter 3

Conditional Logic

Now that you know how to run a program that can complete simple mathematical function, you are ready to move on to a more advanced skill: setting up conditional logic. Once you learn how to run these types of programs, you will be able to set up a program that can have multiple different outcomes depending on the input value. This allows you to create a program that can accomplish more tasks with fewer lines of code.

Here are some terms you will need to know for this chapter:

Conditional Operators: These are mathematical symbols that help determine the value range of a certain number. For example, the equal sign (=) indicates that two numbers or a variable and a number have the same value. Some other conditional operators include not equal (<>), greater than or equal (>=), less than or equal (<=), greater than (>), less than (<) etc.

Logical Operators: Use logical operators when you want to state more than one condition in the same code. Use the word "NOT" to test if the variable does not meet the condition, use "AND" to test for multiple true conditions, use "OR" to test for multiple conditions where only one is true.

You might remember from your early English classes that conditions are If/Then statements. One example of a basic condition is the following sentence: *if* I wake up early *then* I will get to work on time. Lots of popular programing languages rely on conditional statements to complete functions. For example, we can run a program that will check a data list for certain numbers and *if* the program finds those numbers, *then* the program will produce a certain outcome. As a practice, let's create a code that will sort through a list of data, write a word one cell to the right of the data and highlight the number in yellow if it is larger than 5.

How To Set Up A Basic Conditional Logic Program:

1- Begin by creating a list of data. In cells A1-A10, list random integers between 0 and 10. This is a sample data list we will use to test our conditional logic program.

2- Next, open the Visual Basic Editor. Instructions on how to do this can be found in Chapter 2. All new programs will require that you open the Visual Basic Editor.

3- Begin a new Sub and title it "DataSet1"

4- We will begin this program by creating and defining the value of a variable. First type "Dim FirstNumber As Integer". Remember that "FirstNumber" is the name that we have assigned to the variable; however, you could give it any name that you want.

5- Next, we want to define the value of the variable. For this program, we want the value of the variable to be the number that appears in the cells A1 through A10. To do that. we should type "FirstNumber=ActiveCell.Value". This will create a program that whatever cell we have clicked on, VBA will run the program using the number written in that cell for the value of "FirstNumber". For example, if I had typed "8" in cell A1, when I run the program for cell A1, the value of "FirstNumber" becomes 8.

6- Next, we want to set up a conditional logic sequence. We will start by using the word "If" and then type out our condition using a conditional operator. For example, if I wanted to create a

16

program that would check for a certain value range of the selected cell, I might write, "If FirstNumber >= 5".

7- Next, we want to create the condition. On the same line of code write "Then." Your line should look like this: If FirstNumber >=5 Then???

8- After this line of code, set up the condition. Let's say we wanted to have a word appear next to the selected cell if the condition was true. Write ActiveCell (1,2).Value = "Complete". You will notice that (1,2) appears in parenthesis. The "1" indicates the row number and the "2" indicate the column. ActiveCell(1,2) means that I've indicated the same row as the "FirstNumber" value but one column to the right.

9- In addition to adding a word to the right of the number, I also want to highlight the cell that contains the number in yellow. To do this, I will add another line of code: ActiveCell(1,1).Interior.Color=RGB(225,225,0)

A note about colors: In VBA programming, all colors are a combination of Red (notated in the code by the capital R), Green (G), and Blue (B). The most saturated a color can be is indicated by the number 225. Therefore, if the code reads "RGB(0,150,0)", you would have a less saturated color green. If all three numbers are put at 225, the color is black, and if all 3 numbers are 0 then the color is white. You can play around with different number combinations to see what kinds of colors you can make.

10- After you have written the code, you will want to end with the words "End If" and "End Sub". Your code should look something like this:

Sub DataSet1 ()

Dim FirstNumber As Integer

```
FirstNumber=ActiveCell.Value

If FirstNumber>=5 Then

ActiveCell(1,2).Value="Completed"

ActiveCell(1,1).Interior.Color=RGB(225,225,0)

End If

End Sub
```

11- Now, return to the Excel work sheet and highlight cell A1. Run the program and see what happens. If the data in cell A1 met the condition, meaning it was greater than or equal to 5, then the box should have turned yellow and the word "Completed" should have appeared in cell B1. Continue going through your data list running the program for every cell.

The condition we created in this example will only change the worksheet if the data was equal to or greater than 5. But what if we wanted to write a code that would also change the data less than 5? To do this we would need to add a part to our code using Else/ElseIf. Using these terms will help us to write a program that can check for multiple conditions and provide multiple outcomes. Let's try one.

How To Write A Multiple-part Condition:

1- Using the original code from the first practice in this chapter, we are going to add three lines of code. In the line after you indicated the color of the cell write, "ElseIf FirstNumber <5". This will set up the beginning of the second condition the program will check.

2- Now you can choose two new outcomes that will happen if the data is less than 5. For example, you could have a different word appear one cell to write and highlight the data with a different color. Below is a sample code:

18

Active.Cell(1,2).Value= "Not Complete"

ActiveCell (1,1).Interior.Color=RGC(255,0,0)

3- Don't forget to end your code with "End If" and "End Sub".

Here's what the results might look like:

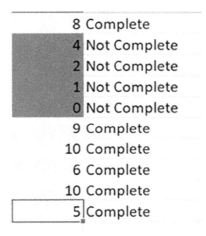

8	Complete
4	Not Complete
2	Not Complete
1	Not Complete
0	Not Complete
9	Complete
10	Complete
6	Complete
10	Complete
5	Complete

Congratulations! You have just created a multi-layered conditional logic program. Before moving on, try running this program a couple more times changing the conditional operator for different results.

Chapter 4

String and String Functions

In this chapter, we will learn how to define variables as strings of text and manipulate that text. To do this, we will define our variable with the phrase "As String." Notice how this is different from the phrase "As Integer" that we have been using in the previous chapters. Let's go over some basic codes that we can use to manipulate text:

LCase: This code allows us to change all the text in a cell to lower case letters.

UCase: This code allows us to change all the text in a cell to upper case letters.

Trim: Use this code when you want to remove or trim extra spaces around or in a line of text.

Space: Use this code when you want to add extra spaces around or in a line of text.

Len: This code will allow you to count how many characters there are in a line of text.

To use any of these functions, type the function's name followed by parenthesis that contains the name of the variable that you want to manipulate. For example, if I had a string of text defined by the variable "String1" and I wanted to trim it I would write, "Trim(String1)". The Space function is slightly different. Instead of including the name of a variable in parenthesis, you will include a number that indicates how many spaces you want and place the variable before or after the Space function. This depends on if you want the space to appear before or after the variable. You will also use the ampersand symbol (&) to combine the variable with the Space function. This symbol (&) is called a concatenation and is used to join two or more things together. For example, the code "Variable1 & Space(5)" will add 5 spaces after the variable while the code "Space(5) & Variable1" will add 5 spaces before the variable.

To practice, we are going to create a series of codes that will complete some of the functions listed above. The first practice will manipulate the letter cases in a list of 5 names. One column to the right the names will be in lower case letters, two columns to the right the names will be in upper case letters, three columns to the right the names will return to proper case (the first letter of both names is capitalized).

How To Create A String Program That Manipulates Letter Cases:

1- Begin by creating a list of five names in a blank Excel spread sheet. Use both the first and last names.

2- Open up the Visual Basic Editor and begin a new Sub. Name the variable "ChangeName" and define it with "As String."

3- Now we will assign a value to the variable. Define the value as "ActiveCell.Value".

4- Now we will have indicated how we want the text manipulated. Let's begin by making all the letters lower case and having that appear one column to the right. To do this, on a new line of code write, "ActiveCell(1,2).Value=LCase(Name)"

5- Now, we will make the letters upper case and appear in the third column. Start a new line of code and write "ActiveCell(1,3).Value=UCase(Name)"

6- Finally, we will have the names return to their proper case in the fourth column. Unfortunately, there is no easy code that will return the names to proper case, but there is a workbook function that will complete the same task. To do this, begin a new line of code and write:

"ActiveCell(1,4).Value=Application.WorksheetFunction.Proper(Name)"

7- When you put all together, your code should look something like this:

```
Sub ChangeName()

Dim Name As String

Name=ActiveCell.Value

ActiveCell(1,2).Value=LCase(Name)

ActiveCell(1,3).Value=UCase(Name)

ActiveCell(1,4).Value=Application.WorksheetFunction.Proper(Name)

End Sub
```

8- Now, return to the Excel spreadsheet. Highlight the name in cell A1 and run the code. Continue and run the code for the names in cells A2 to A5. After you have ran the program, your results might look something like this:

	A	B	C	D	E
1	John Smith	john smith	JOHN SMITH	John Smith	
2	Jane Doe	jane doe	JANE DOE	Jane Doe	
3	Robert Lee	robert lee	ROBERT LEE	Robert Lee	
4	Martha Stewart	martha stewart	MARTHA STEWART	Martha Stewart	
5	Captian Hook	captian hook	CAPTIAN HOOK	Captian Hook	
6					
7					

Congratulations! You just manipulated your first string of text using a program you wrote. Now let's write a program that counts the characters in a string of text.

How To Create A String Program That Counts The Characters In A String:

1- In the same spread sheet, write five more names starting in cell A10.

2- Open the Visual Basic Editor and begin a new Sub.

3- Create a new variable as String and define the value of that variable. For example, your code might say "Dim Name1 As String" and "Name1=ActiveCell.Value"

4- Now, we want to check for any extra spaces in the text. This means we want the program to give us back an integer that tells us how many characters are in the String. We will use the function Len to count the characters. To do this, set up another variable called "Name1Length" and define it as an integer.

5- Next, define the value of "Name1Length" using the function Len. Your code might look something like this:

```
Sub ChangeName2()

Dim Name1 As String

Name1=ActiveCell.Value

Dim Name1Length As Integer

Name1Length=Len(Name1)
```

6- After the program has completed these tasks, we want the program to show us a dialogue box with the answer in it. So, on a new line of code write "MsgBox Name1Length".

7- Return to the Excel spreadsheet and select the name in A10. Run the program. You should have a dialogue box that appears with a number.

If we want to add space or take away space, we would use the functions Trim and Space. Below is a sample code of how you might use these functions. It also uses conditional logic and an addition function.

```
Sub ChangeName3()

Dim Name1 As String

Name1=ActiveCell.Value

ActiveCell(1,2).Value=Name 1 & Space(5)

If ActiveCell(1,2).Value=Name1 & Space(5) Then

Dim Name2 As String

Name2=ActiveCell(1,2).Value

ActiveCell(1,3).Value=Trim(Name2)

End If

MsgBox Len(Name1 + Name2)
```

Now it's your turn. Practice writing a code that can manipulate a string of text. See if you can write a code that also combines functions from the previous chapters.

Chapter 5

String and String Functions [Continued]

In the previous chapter, we learned five basic string functions including LCase, UCase, Trim, Space, and Len. These are only a few of the string functions we can use to manipulate strings of text in an Excel worksheet. In this chapter, we will learn a few more basic string functions that can help us work with strings of text. For example, we can use a string function to replace certain characters in the string, to remove characters from a string, or to reverse a string. Let's take a look at these functions.

Replace: Use this code to replace a string of text with different text. You can replace the entire string or part of the string.

Left: This code cuts characters off of the left side of a string of text.

Right: This code cuts characters off of the right side of a string of text.

StrReverse: This code makes the string of text appear to have been written backwards.

Just like with the string functions described in Chapter 4, you use these functions by typing the function's name followed by parenthesis that contain the name of the variable that you want to manipulate. For example, if I had a string of text defined by the variable "LongString" and I wanted to reverse the order of the characters, I would type "StrReverse(LongString)" to create that program. With the Left and Right functions, you include two things: the variable and how many characters you want to display from either the left or the right of the variable. The Replace function is a bit more complicated. In the parenthesis, you'll need to include three things: first, the main variable that you are searching, the character/string that you want to replace, and the character or string that will become the replacement text. For example, if I had a string of text that had a spelling error in it such as "Reel World" and I wanted to replace one of the "e"s with an "a", I would write the following code with my string defined as the variable "Variable1": Replace(Variable1,"ee","ea")".

Now to practice, we're going to create a series of dialogue boxes that will run these different string functions.

How To Create A String Program That Uses The Replace Function:

1- Begin by opening a new Excel Sheet and writing a list of 5 words starting in cell A1. You will use these words for the practices in this chapter.

2- Open the Visual Basic Editor and set up your Sub by defining the variable as a String and setting the value of the variable.

    Sub ReplaceText()

    Dim Variable1 As String

    Variable1=Range("A1"). Value

3- Now we will write the code for the corrected or replaced text to appear in a message box. In a new line of code, set up a new variable and define it using the Replace function. Be sure to indicate what you want to replace. In my example, the word "Happi" appears in cell A1. I want to replace "Happi" with "Happiness", so I would write the following code:

    Dim CorrectText As String

    CorrectedText=Replace(Variable1,"i","iness")

    MsgBox CorrectedText

26

4- Now run the program. A dialogue box should appear with the replaced word.

If we wanted to both replace the text and then have a dialogue box that showed the replaced text in reverse, we could edit the last line of our code to read:

MsgBox StrReverse(CorrectedText)

With this code, we would be combining two different string functions into one program. The more string functions that you become comfortable using, the more complicated your codes can become. Let's try another practice.

How to create a string program that uses the Left and Right functions:

1- Open the Visual Basic Editor and begin a new Sub. Define the new variable as a string and set its value to A2

Sub LeftRight()

Dim Variable2 As String

Variable2=Range("A2").Value

2- Now, we will create a message box that shows us a string that contains the first and last two letters of the word in cell A2. In my example, I used the word "Delicious," so, when I run the program I want the message box to read "Deus."

3- Set up the new variable as String and define its value using the functions Left and Right

Dim NewWord As String

NewWord=Left(Variable2,2) & Right(Variable2,2)

MsgBox NewWord

4- Run the program. If you are only getting 3 or 2 letters, make sure the word in cell A2 does not have spaces at the end of it since spaces also count as characters.

Congratulations! You have learned the basics of string functions. Try to write your own code that combines the skills learned in Chapter 1 through 5. Make sure to master these skills before moving on to the next section.

Part Two:
For Intermediate Programmers

Chapter 6

Programming Loops

Now that you know the basics of VBA Programming, it's time to learn some new skills. In this chapter, we will learn about Programming Loops, including what they are and how to use them.

What is a Programming Loop?

As its name suggests, a Programming Loop is a program that runs a certain function over and over again (in a loop) until you, the programmer, tell it to stop. Programming Loops can be a bit difficult to understand but going through the following steps will help you grasp the basics of this function.

Why are Programming Loops useful?

Let's say you had a list of data in cells A1 through A100 and you wanted to add all these cells together and find the sum. You could use the addition function and create a code that would add A1+A2+A3 etc. But only using the addition function, you would need to write out every cell and add it up, a process that would take a long time to type out. Instead, you can write a program, that will add A1 and A2, then take the new sum and repeat the process. This is a Programming Loop and it can drastically decrease the time it takes to do simple mathematical functions for long lists of numbers.

There are a few different kinds of Programming Loops. In this chapter, we will go over the first type, For Loop, but for future reference, here are the definitions of each loop function:

For Loop: This programming loop will run the program from top to bottom until it reaches the end condition.

For Each Loop: This programming loop is similar to a For Loop except that it works with collections or arrays (something you will learn about in Chapter 7).

Do While Loop: This programming loop runs in conjunction with conditions (explored in Chapter 3) and will run as long as the condition you set is true. Once the condition is false, the program will stop.

Do Until Loop: Similar to the Do While Loop, this programming loop will run until it finds a false condition. This type of loop will produce a slightly different end result than the Do While Loop, but they are overall very similar.

In this practice, we are going to set up a program that will add the numbers 1 through 10 using a Loop function. Let's get started.

How To Create A Simple Programming Loop:

1- Begin by opening a new Excel spreadsheet and open the Visual Basic Editor.

2- Set up a new Sub and define 3 variables all as Integers. For this Programming Loop you will need a start value, an end value, and an answer.

3- Now, we want to set a limit to the loop or define a place for it to stop. We will use the variable EndValue as our stopping place. Because we want the loop to end once it has added the numbers 1 through 10, 10 becomes the value of EndValue.

4- Now that the end parameter is defined, we can write the Programming Loop. For this program, we will be using the For Loop function. Begin a new line of code and write "For" then add the variable that will be the start value. Define the value of that start value.

For StartValue=1

5- Now we are going to finish the loop. Write the word "To". This defines how long the loop will run. Since we've already set the end value using the variable EndValue, type "EndValue" next. Your code might look something like this:

For StartValue=1 To EndValue

6- Notice that the StartValue in the Loop function has to be defined as a variable. For example, it might make sense to define the value of each variable and then set up a Loop function like this:

StartValue=1

EndValue=10

For StartValue To EndValue

However, if you wrote this code, it would give you an error message because VBA requires a variable to start the Programming Loop.

7- After we have defined the parameters of the Loop function, we want to introduce the mathematical function that the program will execute. Do this by using the third variable "Answer". Write a new line of code that says "Answer=Answer+StartValue"

8- Now we want a dialogue box to appear after the program??? runs every step of the program???. Write a new line of code that reads "MsgBox Answer"

9- Next, we will tell the program to repeat the Loop. Write "Next" followed by the start value variable.

32

10- After the program has run through the set number of loops, we want another dialogue box to appear that says "You Did It!" Code this dialogue box.

11- Together your code might look something like this:

```
Sub LoopPractice()

Dim StartValue As Integer

Dim EndValue As Integer

Dim Answer As Integer

EndNumber=10

For StartNumber=1 To EndNumber

Answer=Answer+StartNumber

MsgBoxAnswer

Next StartNumber

MsgBox "You Did It!"

End Sub
```

12- Run the program. 10 dialogue boxes should appear that contain the answers to the summed numbers up to that point in the program. After the 10th box, a final dialogue box will appear that says "You Did It!"

Congratulations! You just ran your first Programming Loop. Now, see if you can change your code to run with different start and end values or use a different Programming Loop function to see what kinds of results you might get.

Chapter 7

Programming Arrays

In the last chapter, you learned how to create a basic Programming Loop. One way to make Programming Loops more useful is to use them in conjunction with Programming Arrays.

What is a Programming Array?

In the previous chapters of this book, whenever you store the data of a variable, it can only be a singular value, such as one integer or one string of text. A Programming Array allows you to store more than one value in the same variable.

You set up a Programming Array similar to the way that you set up any other variable, except you add parenthesis after the name of the variable that defines how many spaces there are for storing data. Then you have to create a list that outlines what data is stored in each space. For example, to set up a simple Programming Array, your code might look like this:

```
Sub ProgrammingArrayPractice()

Dim Variable(4) As Integer

Variable(0)=0

Variable(1)=1

Variable(2)=2

Variable(3)=3

Variable(4)=4
```

Notice that we indicated that the variable has a subscript of 4 but that there are 5 spaces to store data. That's because by writing 4 we have indicated that there is a space in the following numbers: 0,1,2,3,4. VBA automatically includes 0. If you want to exclude 0, just define the variable in a different way.

Dim Variable(1 To 5) As Integer

Now let's try using a Programming Array together with a Programming Loop.

How To Set Up A Programming Array:

1- Open up an Excel spreadsheet and open the Visual Basic Editor.

2- Begin a new Sub and name it "ArrayPractice"

3- Next, set up your array variable. You can either select a number or a range. Indicate that the array variable is an integer so that you can use mathematical functions in conjunction with your array variable. They might look something like this:

Variable(1)= 100

Variable(2)= 150

Variable(3)= Variable(1)*Variable(2)

Variable(4)= 600

Variable(5)= Variable(3)+Variable(4)

4- After you have defined the value of the array variable, set up the value of each array.

5- Now set up the loop function. We will use a simple For Loop to place all of the variables in a table in the Excel Spread sheet. Set up the Loop function by writing "For" now we are going to define the starting variable using the letter "X" where "X=1" we

36

will set the parameters of the loop function as "UBound(Variable)". This indicates that we will run the function through the uppermost bound variable, or Variable(5).

6- Next, we want to set these values into spreadsheet cells. To do this, write, "Cell(x,1).Value=Variable(X)". This means that whatever number variable the loop works through, it will place the value in the x row and the 1 column.

7- Finally, close the Loop by writing "Next X".

8- Put together, your code might look like this:

```
Sub ArrayPractice()

Dim Varaible(1 To 5) As Integer

Variable(1)= 100

Variable(2)= 150

Variable(3)= Variable(1)*Variable(2)

Variable(4)= 600

Variable(5)= Variable(3)+Variable(4)

For X=1 To UBound(Variable)

Cells(X,1).Value=Variable(X)

Next X

End Sub
```

9- Run the program. If you used the numbers in the example above, you might have something that looks like this:

	A	B
1	100	
2	150	
3	15000	
4	600	
5	15600	
6		
7		
8		

Congratulations! You just created your first Programming Array. Now try defining different array variables in your code and seeing what kinds of results you can get.

Chapter 8

Subs and Functions

So far in this book, we have learned how to create Subs. However, there are other ways to create code as well. One way is to create a Function. In this chapter, we will learn a bit more about how Subs are formatted and then, we will learn how to create a Function.

What is a Sub?

A Sub is a short, coded program that will perform a specific task. So far, we've been running the Subs from the "run" button in the Visual Basic Editor. However, you can also run Subs with the shortcut F5 or you can create a button in the worksheet to run a Sub. And finally, you can run a Sub from another Sub.

Adding a button is fairly easy. All you do is go to the "Developer" tab and click on "Insert." After that, a drop-down menu will open up. Click on the first icon in the first row. This will pull up a dialogue box that will ask you to select what Sub you want the button to correspond to. After that, click on the spreadsheet where you want the button to appear. Now, any time you press that particular button, it will run the specific Sub. You can also rename the button by clicking on the text that appears in the button's center.

Running a Sub from another Sub is a bit more complicated. We use conditional logic to set up a condition of when to call up the other Sub. Let's do a practice.

How To Run A Sub From Another Sub:

1- Begin by opening up a new Excel spreadsheet. Open the Visual Basic Editor and begin a new Sub. We're going to being by setting up the Sub that will run the second Sub.

2- Name the Sub and then define the variable as an integer.

3- After you have defined the variable, set the value of the variable. For this program, we are going to set the value as "ActiveCell.Value".

4- Next, set up a condition. For this program, we are going to change the font of a number if it is less than 10. So far, your code might look something like this:

> Sub Program1()
>
> Dim Variable1 As Integer
>
> Variable1=ActiveCell.Value
>
> If Variable1 <10 Then

5- To finish the end of the condition, we are going to use the function "Call". We are going to call a second Sub. In a new line write, "Call Program2". Finish the first Sub by writing "End If" and "End Sub".

6- Now we are going to write the second Sub. Begin a new sub and title it "Program2".

7- To set up this next program, type "With ActiveCell. Font" since we want to change the font of numbers less than 20. In a new line, write the types of font changes you want to see. Your code might look something like this:

```
Sub Program2()

With ActiveCell.Font

.Bold= True

.Name= "Helvetica"

.Size= "18"

End With

End Sub
```

8- After both of the codes are written, run the program. The font size and type should change for numbers less than 10. Here's what the code looks like put together:

What is a Function?

Functions are very similar to Subs. The only difference is that a Sub will not provide a tangible outcome, like a dialogue box, unless we write that into the program. Subs also do not store the results that they obtain anywhere in their coding. Functions, on the other hand, are able to obtain a return value and then store this value within the program so that they can recall the information later.

Excel worksheets also have many built-in functions that you can access through VBA programming. For example, let's say we have a data set that we want Excel to find the sum of. To do this, we would write a program utilizing a Worksheet Function. Let's try a practice:

How To Execute Worksheet Functions:

1- Open a new Excel workbook and create a data set. Have the data set fill at least cells A1 to A10.

2- Open the Visual Basic Editor and start a new code. Set up a Function program by typing "Function" and the name of the new program variable.

3- Next, define the variable as an Integer or Long depending on the size of data you are working with.

4- Now, we will define the value of the variable using a Worksheet Function. Since we want to find the sum of a list of data, we write, "Variable1=WorsheetFunction.Sum(Range("A1": "A10"))". Make sure to close both sets of parentheses.

5- Next, we will indicate in what cell to place the data from the Variable. Write, "Range("A11").Value=Variable1". We can also place the word "Sum" in a cell. Your code might look something like this:

Function SumTotal()

42

```
Dim Variable1 As Long

Variable1=WorksheetFunction.Sum(Range("A1:A10"))

Range("A11").Value=Variable1

Range("B11").Value= "Sum"

End Function
```

6- Run the program. In cell A11 you should see the answer and in cell B11 the word "sum" should appear.

Explore a few more of Excel's Worksheet Functions. Once you type in the words "WorksheetFunction.", a list of worksheet functions should appear. See if you recognize any from Excel's normal functions.

Chapter 9

Writing and Recording Macros

One of the most useful parts of VBA programing is the ability to create a Macro. Simply put, a Macro is a program that can automatically run any Excel task. This means that instead of typing in each keystroke every time you want to perform a simple task, you can program a Macro and it will run the task for you. Using Macros will drastically decrease the time you spend typing out commands and increase your overall efficiency.

If you have been following through the practices in each chapter, you have already created many Macros. Each short Sub or Function that you have created works as a Macro, thereby automating Excel tasks through coded language. In this chapter, you will learn how to record a Macro through the Excel workbook.

There are two ways to create a Macro in VBA. First, you can program the Macro yourself or you can record a Macro. Recording a Macro is simple.

How to record a Macro:

1- On the Developer's tab, find the button that says "Record Macro"

2- Click on this button to begin recording a Macro. It will open up a dialogue box that will ask you to name the new Macro being recorded. Remember to name it something explanatory so that you can find it later.

3- Next, perform any function that you want in the Excel worksheet. This might include changing the color of a certain cell, finding the sum of a list of data, or creating a new table.

4- Once you have performed the task you want to be recorded, click the "Stop Recording" button.

Congratulations! You have just recorded your first Macro. Recording Macros can be helpful if you do not yet know how to program the Macro yourself. However, it does have limitations. For example, it cannot run through Loops. Also, the Macro recorder often uses much more coding than is necessary and can ultimately slow down your process. All in all, it is more beneficial to learn how to program the Macro yourself.

Chapter 9

Excel Objects

Excel Objects refer to the parts that comprise the Excel workbook, including the rows and columns, the cell ranges, the worksheets, and the workbooks. Every Excel Object has certain properties that Excel stores as part of it. For example, a cell's properties might include the font, the font size and type, the color of the cell and the data stored in the cell. The worksheet has different properties, including its name, how much protection has been placed on it (such as a password), and its scroll area. In Chapter 3, we learned how to change a cell's color by accessing one of its properties: "ActiveCell(1,1).Interior.Color".

The Visual Basic Editor on the left side column will often contain a list of the selected object's properties:

Properties - Sheet1	✕
Sheet1 Worksheet	▾

Alphabetic | Categorized

(Name)	Sheet1
DisplayPageBreaks	False
DisplayRightToLeft	False
EnableAutoFilter	False
EnableCalculation	True
EnableFormatConditic	True
EnableOutlining	False
EnablePivotTable	False
EnableSelection	0 - xlNoRestrictions
Name	Sheet1
ScrollArea	
StandardWidth	8.09
Visible	-1 - xlSheetVisible

Here are definitions for a few of the most common Objects:

Application: These types of objects are top level objects because they are connected to the host program, Excel. VBA can also access programs outside Excel such as Microsoft Word and PowerPoint. You can learn more about that in Chapter 15. This work can often be omitted when writing a program because it is implied.

Workbook: This object controls workbook tasks such as opening and closing, saving, or creating a new workbook. It can appear in code as both a singular and a plural word, either "ActiveWorkbook" or "ActiveWorkbooks" in your program.

Worksheet: This is one of the most common objects because the most common programs manipulate the functions of a single worksheet. So far in this book, we have only created programs that produce results with one worksheet. Again, this word can be both singular and plural, either "ActiveWorksheet" or "ActiveWorksheets".

Range: This type of object refers to a cell or section of cells, rows and columns. It works in conjunction with Worksheets.

Using Excel Objects allows your program to have total control over Excel's functions and an object's properties. Let's practice by opening, renaming, and saving a workbook.

How to use the Workbook Object:

1- Begin by creating a new Excel Workbook. Name it "Object Practice," save it and close it.

2- Next, open a new Excel Workbook and open the Visual Basic Editor.

3- Begin a new Sub and title it "OpenWorkbook"

4- Now we are going to open a workbook from within the Visual Basic Editor. First, identify the Object "Workbooks" then type a period and the function "Open".

5- On the same line of code, call up the file name. You can do this by typing "Filename:= "Object Practice". The symbol used here (:=) is called an assignment operator.

6- Run the code. The Excel Workbook named "Object Practice" will open.

7- Close "Object Practice" and return to the Visual Basic Editor. Next, we will add to our code to save the Excel Workbook "Object Practice" with a new name.

8- After the lines of code you just wrote, begin a new Sub and title it "SaveWorkbook".

9- In a new line of code, identify the object again "Workbooks" but now we will identify the specific object in a parenthetical statement. Write "Workbooks("Object Practice")". After you have identified the object, type a period and identify the function "SaveAs" or "Save". After a space, type the new name of the workbook. In my example, I chose "New Object Practice".

10- Run the code. The Excel workbook "Object Practice" will open and have a new name "New Object Practice".

11- In total, your code might look something like this:

Sub OpenWorkbook()

Workbooks.Open Filename:= "Object Practice"

End Sub

Sub SaveWorkbook()

```
Workbooks("Object   Practice").SaveAs   "New   Object
Practice"

End Sub
```

Congratulations! You just learned how to access Excel Objects through
the Visual Basic Editor. Continue practicing the skills learned in this
section before moving on.

Part Three:
For Advanced Programmers

Chapter 11

Excel Events

In Excel VBA, an event refers to any incident that occurs while working in Excel, whether in the Visual Basic Editor or the spreadsheet itself. Since this definition is so broad, you might wonder why dedicate an entire chapter to explain how Excel Events work? Well, one feature of VBA is that you can program Macros that are triggered by certain events. For example, if you are filling out a data table, once you have filled 10 cells, a Macro could run that would automatically put the sum of the data in the next cell. This makes using Excel spreadsheets super easy and efficient. By learning how to use events to trigger macros, you will be able to increase the interactivity of Excel worksheets as well as improve the overall user experience.

When creating automatically executed programs, you generally use a Sub procedure. Note that Function procedures are not often triggered by events. Using events is also important when programming User Forms. You will learn more about that in Chapter 12.

In order to practice learning about events, we are going to create a program that will run with the click of a button.

How To Run A Program Triggered By An Event:

1- Open a new Excel workbook and open the Visual Basic Editor.

2- Create a new Sub and write a program. You can use one of the programs from another chapter in this book or one of the programs that you wrote as practices. In this practice, I'm going to write in a basic dialogue box to appear at the click of a button. My code looks something like this:

Sub Event1()

MsgBox "You Can VBA Program!"

End Sub

3- Once you have the program written, assign it to a button. Return to the Excel spreadsheet and find the "Developer" tab. Select insert and then the "button" option. It is the first symbol on the first line of the drop-down menu when you click "Insert" as seen in the image below.

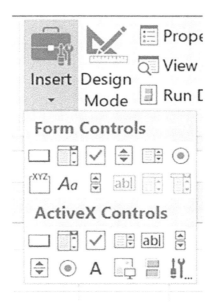

4- Click on the spreadsheet where you want the upper-left corner of the button to appear and drag it until it is the desired size, usually about 2 cells over and 2 cells down.

5- Next, you will be prompted to select a Macro to assign to this button. Select the Macro that you just created in step 2 of this practice.

6- Now, click on your newly-created button. The program will run. If you used my program above, a dialogue box with the words "You Can VBA Program!" will appear.

Congratulations! You just used an event (the click of a button) to trigger a Macro. See what other programs you can attach to buttons in your worksheet.

Chapter 12

VBA Error Types

When working in Excel VBA, as with any other coding program, you will definitely run into errors. Even experienced coders often receive error messages on their codes. The Visual Basic Editor tries to catch all errors before you even attempt to run the program. For example, if you have an error in a line of code you just wrote, an error message will appear if you try to move onto the next line of code. This can be helpful because it will help you catch any errors only seconds after they were made. In general, the errors you might run into while writing VBA programs can be broken down into three categories: syntax errors, runtime errors, and logical errors.

Syntax Errors

A syntax error, also known as a compile error, includes anything in the code that is typed incorrectly. This includes things such as a missing parenthesis, an undefined variable or having too many parts, as is illustrated by the error message below.

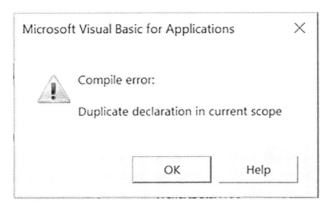

This type of error occurs at the time of interpretation. In other words, as soon as VBA detects a syntax error in your code, an error message will let you know. The Visual Basic Editor will usually highlight the line that has the error in it in either red font or with a yellow arrow to the side of the line. The best way to fix a syntax error is to carefully read the error message and determine if something is missing, mistyped, or added. Often times, it helps to rewrite the line entirely from scratch. If you are still receiving and error code, have another person who is familiar with VBA programming look at your code. Often times, it is hard to catch small errors like missing periods or parenthesis. But if someone else looks at your code with fresh eyes, they will often be able to spot the error.

Runtime Errors

Runtime errors, or exceptions, include anything in the code that VBA cannot execute such as a variable that does not fit properly into the code, a function that does not exist or a mathematical task that cannot be performed such as dividing by zero. Unlike syntax errors (which will appear while writing the code), this type of error occurs at the time of execution. That means that after you run the program if you code contains a runtime error, an error message will occur. A few common runtime errors include error number nine: "subscript out of range." Receiving an error message like this indicates that your code tries to obtain a number in a range you have not indexed. Another common error is number thirteen: "type mismatch." This error message means that you have defined your variable incorrectly. For example, you may have defined your variable as an integer, but you want it to produce a number larger than 32,696 so you will need to use "Long" instead.

Runtime errors are usually easy to correct because VBA will provide you with a dialogue box that explains the nature of the error. Additionally, in some versions of the Visual Basic Editor, the dialogue box that explains the error will also provide you with the option to

"Debug" your program. Clicking on this box will highlight the line in your code that is causing the error message to occur.

Logical Errors

Logical errors are identified by many coders as being the most difficult type of error. Also known as "bugs," these types of errors do not hinder VBA's ability to run the program. However, you will know that an error has occurred if the program you ran produced unexpected results or deviated from the course that you programed. For example, you may have reversed the order of your variables, so that the program was performing the wrong function for each one. VBA did not detect anything wrong with the program and therefore did not produce and error message because it was still able to perform the function.

In order to correct a logical error, you need to carefully review your code to pinpoint what went wrong. This can be difficult, especially for beginning programmers, but VBA has a few tools to help you debug your code. If you left click on the grey bar to the left of your programming window, a red dot will appear. This is called a "Breakpoint." Setting a "Breakpoint" will run the code up until this point and then from here you can either check the value of your variables, run the code line by line, or pause the program altogether. Checking the value of a variable is easy. Simply hover your curser over the variable you want to verify and a small box will appear below with the value written. If you want to pause the program or run through it line by line, use the "Debug" tab in the Visual Basic Editor window and select either "Step Into" or "Step Over." The option "Step Into" will run every line of code. "Step Over" will do the same, except it will step over or exclude other parts of the program called up by the current code.

Chapter 13

Excel VBA and User Forms

One of the important functions of Excel VBA Programming is the ability to create user forms. Custom-made forms can look very impressive. Additionally, with user forms, you no longer have to be the only one responsible for imputing data into the Excel worksheet. Anyone who has access to the user form will be able to fill it out and, through VBA Programming, the Excel worksheet will be automatically filled out. However, there are a few downsides to user forms. For example, you cannot guarantee that the person filling out the user form is doing so correctly and there may be errors.

In order to create a functioning user form, there are two parts: first, creating the form and second, programming the form. In this chapter, we will learn how to create the form in the Visual Basic Editor. The next chapter will explain how to write the program so that the form can be used.

How To Create A User Form:

1- Open up a new Excel Workbook and open the Visual Basic Editor.

2- Once in the VB Editor, find the "Insert" tab. Click on it. This will pull up a short menu with one of the options being "Userforms." Select to insert a "Userform".

3- After selecting this option, a new window will appear in your coding area that looks like this:

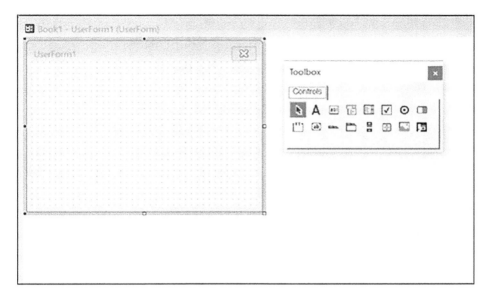

4- The work area contains a dotted grey area as well as a tool box. To create the user form, we will use certain parts of the toolbox.

5- We will begin by creating a simple button. To do that, select the "CommandButton" option. In the image above, it is the second icon on the second row that has the small "ab" characters inside it. Once you have this option selected, click on the grey work space where you want the upper left corner of the button to appear and drag your cursor until it fills up the space you want the entire button to occupy.

6- After you have created a button, a list of properties will appear in the left-hand column. To see an example of this list, reference Chapter 10. From this list, you can easily change the name of the button, its color, the font of the text, its position in the form, or any of the other listed properties.

7- Next, we will create a text box. In the image above, the "Textbox" button is the third one in the first row. Click on this button and repeat the same process as with creating the command button. Once again, you can access all the properties of the textbox on the left-hand menu.

8- Once you have added both a command button and a textbox to your user form, run the program. Your custom-made user form will appear. However, nothing will happen when you click the button or write in the text box space. This is because the user form is not yet attached to any specific program.

Now that we have created a form, we need to attach a program to it for it to be useful.

How To Program A User Form:

1- Return to the Visual Basic Editor where you created the user form. We'll begin by adding code to the button. To do this, double click on the button in the creating space. This will pull up a separate window that is already set up to run a "Private Sub".

2- You will notice that at the top of this new work space, there are two drop down menus. One lists the name of the button we are coding for and the other says "Click." If you click on this second menu, you will see a drop-down list of all the different events that could happen with this button. Click is the default setting for buttons, but you could select any number of events to activate this code. You will notice that the name of this "Private Sub" appears as "CommandButton1_Click". You can code for any of the events simply by replacing the word "Click" in the code with a different event.

3- We want whatever value typed into the textbox to appear in an active cell. To do this we would write the following code: "ActiveCell.Value=TextBox1.Text". Notice that we placed the name of the textbox, "TextBox1", as the value of the active cell. We also indicated that we wanted to use the property "Text", so that appears after the period.

4- Finally, we want the use form to disappear once we have input the data. We do this by using the keyword "Unload" followed by the name of the form or the word "Me".

5- Your final code might look something like this:

Private Sub CommandButton1_Click()

ActiveCell.Value=TextBox1.Text

Unload Me

End Sub

Congratulations! You just created your first user form with an attached program. Keep practicing by exploring the user form creator and seeing how else you can manipulate the spreadsheet. You could try to change the color of the active cell or add the answer to a mathematical function. See what you can do and keep practicing.

Chapter 14

Connect with External Data

E xcel workbooks have the ability to connect with external data, which is data that is stored outside of the workbook itself. This data could be stored in another Excel workbook or other Microsoft programs, such as Microsoft Word or Microsoft Access. Additionally, you can access data stored in SQL server tables. There are many options.

A simple way to connect to these external data sources is to use the "Data" tab found in the main toolbar.

Once you open the "Data" tab, the first option on the left-hand side allows you to choose from multiple sources of external data. From this tab, you can set up an external connection and run it. Connecting to external data is an important part of Excel because it allows you to easily input large amounts of data without having to manually enter each set. If the connection between the Excel spreadsheet and the data base remains strong, then you can easily "Refresh" the data and see the new input data from the "Data" tab.

You can also use VBA Programming to write a program that will connect to external data. The coding required for this kind of program is quite advanced. As a practice, we are going to combine the data from 3 separate Excel spreadsheets into one table. Before running through this practice, create 3 separate Excel spreadsheets that contain rows of data from cell A1 through C10, or a different range, but be sure to change that range in the following code.

How to combine data in Excel:

1- Begin by setting up a sub and defining the variables. In this practice we will have 8 separate variables:
   a. For creating an Array that contains the names of the source files
      Dim SourceArray
   b. To name the specific sheet from which we are pulling the data
      Dim SheetName As String
   c. To name the range on the specific sheet from which we are pulling the data
      Dim SourceRange As String
   d. To be sure we pull the data from the entire sheet
      Dim LastRow as Long
   e. To name the new workbook where we will combine the data
      Dim TargetWorkbook As Workbook
   f. To name the sheet in the workbook where we will combine the data
      Dim TargetSheet As Workbook
   g. To open the new workbook where we will combine the data and run the program
      Dim sourceFile As Workbook
   h. To stand in place of all three file names in a single line of code
      Dim X as Integer

2- After defining these variables, we will create the path where the data will travel. In place of "file1" etc. you will include the name of the file where the data is originally stored. All Excel file names will look something like this: "E:\file1.xlsx"
   SourceArray=Array("file1", "file2", "file3")

3- Next, name the Sheet in which you will be inputting the data:
   SheetName= "Combined Data"

4- In this next step, we will indicate the range of cells in which the original data is stored. For example, if the data was stored in

63

columns A through C in rows 1 through 10, then my code would look like this: SourceRange= "A1:C10"

5- Next, write a code to open a new workbook:

```
Set TargetWorkbook=Worbooks.Add
```

6- Now, write a code to indicate in which workbook you will be adding the data.

```
Set   TargetSheet=TargetWorkbook.Sheets("Combined Data")
```

7- Next, we will write the code that indicates for every file we open, stored in variable X, we will collect the data up until the last row of data stored

```
For X=0 To UBound(SourceArray)
Set sourceFile=Workbooks.Open(SourceArray(X))
LastRow=TargetSheet.Cells(TargetSheet.Rows.Count, 1). End(xlUp).Row
```

8- The next part of this code indicates that you will copy all the data into the indicated worksheet, defined by variable "TargetSheet", then close the files in which the data was originally stored.

```
With sourceFile
.Sheets(SheetName).Range(SourceRange).Copy
Destination:=TargetSheet.Range("A" & LastRow +1)
.Close
End With
```

9- After gathering the data and pasting it into the new worksheet, you can now save the worksheet under a new name.

```
Next
TargetWorkbook.SaveAs "Collected Data Updated"
```

10- End the Sub and run the program.

As you can see, writing this program requires the use of many different elements of the chapters that we have gone over. We defined 8 variables, including an Array variable. We also accessed built-in Excel object properties and defined ranges. With practice, and as you become more familiar will all the functions and properties that are available through Excel VBA, you will be able to write and run complex programs that can automate many parts of Microsoft Excel.

Conclusion

Congratulations! You have completed the final chapter of *Excel VBA: Step-by-Step Guide To Learn And Master Excel VBA Programming*. I hope the lessons you found in this book were informative and able to provide you with all of the tools you need to master VBA programming. Remember, learning a new skill can be hard work—especially, learning a new coding language—but if you follow these step-by-step practices, it will be easier to reach your goals. Each program you write is a victory!

In order to continue learning VBA Programming, it's important that you continue writing code and making mistakes. The best way to learn about VBA Programming, as you have found by working through the chapters in this book, is to practice. Get into the Visual Basic Editor and explore all the different functions and properties that Excel has to offer. Making mistakes and learning how to resolve them is also an important part of the learning process. As you discover the different options and make a few mistakes along the way, you will be coding like a pro in no time.

Finally, if you found this book helpful, then I'd like to ask you for a favor. Would you be kind enough to leave a review for this book on Amazon? It'd be greatly appreciated!

Thank you and good luck!

Excel VBA

Top Tips, Tricks, Timesavers, and Common Mistakes in VBA Programming

Introduction

Congratulations on purchasing *Excel VBA*, and thank you for doing so. VBA, for those who don't know, stands for Visual Basic for Applications. This is a Microsoft-implemented, event-driven programming language—i.e. this is Microsoft Office's personal programming language.

There are many different things that you can do with VBA in Excel, which include:

1. Creating Macros – Excel VBA allows you to automate tasks by writing what they call macros.

2. MsgBox – This is a dialog box that can be used to inform a user of your program.

3. Worksheet and Workbook Objects

4. Range Objects – This is an important part of VBA because it represents the cells in your worksheet.

5. Variables

6. If Then Statements – These are used to let the program know when to execute a line of code once conditions have been met.

7. Loops – This has to be the best technique that you can use. Loops in VBA allows you to loop through different cells with a few code lines.

8. String Manipulation – These are the important functions to manipulate strings.

These are just a few things that can be done with Excel VBA. This book will look at many different things to help you do these tasks and more. Everything in this book is meant to help you perform faster and more efficiently, so let's get started.

There are plenty of books on this subject on the market; thanks again for choosing this one! Every effort was made to ensure it is full of as much useful information as possible. Please enjoy!

Tips, Tricks, and Timesavers

Immediate Window

This first tip will explain how you can use the immediate window in the debugging environment in VBA for Excel. Immediate window is used to debug a program by letting you enter and run a code in the suspended program.

The immediate window is especially helpful when you have to find out the value of an object, expression, or variable at a certain place in your program. You can do this by using the Print command.

If you are interested in checking the current values of a variable that we'll call pValue, you can use the Print command. For this example, you will type "*print pValue*" in your immediate window and select enter.

Your immediate window should display the result in the following line. What you get will depend on your code. You can even choose to type in more complicated expressions into your immediate window; just end it by pressing Enter.

For example, you can type in "*print Mid(pValue, LPos, 1)*". After you hit enter, you will get a response from the immediate window.

The immediate window is also able to run at different types of VBA code, but remember that the immediate window can only word when debugging—i.e. any code you run is only for debugging. The code you type in here will not be saved to your existing code.

Recorder

One of the amazing tools in Excel VBA is the macro recorder. This recorder registers each task that you perform with Excel. The only thing you have to do is a record a certain task one time. The next time that you do it, you can execute the task over and over with just one click. The macro recorder is also helpful when you're unsure of how to program a certain task. All you have to do is open the Visual Basic Editor after you record your task so that you can see how it can be programmed.

The downside is that there are several things that you can't do with the macro recorder. For example, a macro can't be used to loop through a data range. Moreover, the recorder uses way more code than you need to, which can end up slowing down your process.

To record a macro:

1. While on the Developer tab, select Record Macro.

2. Enter your name for the macro into the specified field on the form.

3. In the store macro from the drop-down menu, select This Workbook. By doing this, your macro will only be stored in your current workbook.

Note: if you end up saving the macro into the personal macro workbook, your macro will then be available for you to use in all of your workbooks. This is possible since Excel saves all of the macros in a hidden workbook that will automatically open when Excel is started. If you keep all of your macros in a New Workbook, the macro is only going to be accessible in a newly opened workbook.

4. Now, select OK.

5. Next, right-click (mouse) on your active cell. Make sure that you don't select any other ones. Then, click Format Cells.

6. Go down and select Percentage.

7. Select OK.

8. Lastly, select Stop Recording.

Now, you have recorded your first macro with the macro recorder.

It's important that you test the macro to make sure that you can change the number format to percentage. To do so, perform the following steps:

1. Type in a few numbers between 0 and 1.

2. Select all of the cells with these numbers.

3. Back on the Developer tab, click on Macros.

4. Select Run.

5. Then, look at the results you get. Your decimal points should have been changed into percentages.

If you want to look at your macro, open the Visual Basic Editor. Your macro will have been placed into a module labeled module1. When a code is located in a module, it means that it is available for the entire workbook. This means that you are able to choose Sheet2 or Sheet3 and change numbers in cells on those sheets, too. Keep in mind that the codes that are placed on the sheet and assigned a command button to will only be available for that specific sheet.

Debug.Print

Knowing how to debug a program is an important skill when it comes to software development. Understanding VBA's debugging tools makes the development easier and more productive.

The most common way for people to debug a code is to step through it line-by-line. In order to do this:

1. Place your cursor on the first line that you want to be analyzed, then select F8, or pick Step Into on your debug menu.

2. The code lines on deck to be executed will be highlighted in color yellow. These highlighted lines are yet to be executed.

If the code you have calls a different procedure, when you step through with F8, it will make the execution enter that procedure in this series. If you choose to execute it without using the stepping-through feature, upon pressing SHIFT F8, it would execute that procedure and then stop at the end of that line once it has been called.

When you are stepping through, CTRL F8 can be used to resume your line-by-line execution. During times that your execution gets paused because of a breakpoint or a step-by-step mode, you are able to hit Continue or F5 while in the Run menus to make VBA finish its run—or until it hits another pause.

A breakpoint is a marker that has been added to the code that will make the execution of the code to immediately pause before it executes the next line. You can add in a breakpoint by placing the cursor on the code line that you want to place a breakpoint in. Afterwards, click F9, then select Toggle Breakpoint on the debug menu. Another option is to click on the left margin beside the line of code. Once you have set a breakpoint, the line will be shown in a red background. When you run that particular code, it will pause the execution right before this line, and it will be displayed with a yellow background.

With VBA, you will get debug objects that come with two different properties—assert and print. You can use these to show a variable's value so that you can control its flow in your program. Debug. Print will place everything that comes after it into the immediate window. The execution of the code won't be interrupted. Once it has displayed the text in your immediate window, the execution of the code will finish its run. You will also have the ability to mix actual text into the variable names when you create a Debug. Print statement, such as:

"Debug.Print "The value of variable Y is: " & Y"

You are also able to display several variables at a single time in your immediate window by placing commas between them, such as:

"Debug.Print X, Y, Z'

It's important that you remove or comment out your Debug. Print statements once you have finished debugging your code. You won't typically want these to be operative during the code's normal usage.

Reducing Workbook Size

If you are experienced in using Excel, you've probably encountered really large file sizes. These things are terrible. They are hard to email to customers or colleagues, they take a really long time to open, and they will take forever to update or change any of the formulas every time you have to change something.

This means that you are stuck sitting in front of a loading bar, wasting time, when you could be finishing up your work. How did these things get so unworkable and big? If they are being shared with others, chances are you won't find out.

There are many different ways to fix this within Excel.

- Get rid of "blank space" within the sheets.

This is typically the most common reason for a large file size and is the easiest to fix. Excel has a "used range" for each workbook sheet. The large this is, the larger your file size will be.

While in an Excel workbook, if you press Ctrl + End, you will get a "last used cell." If this places you several rows or columns past your data, all of those cells are upping your file size.

To Fix:

1. Click on the first blank column or row. A shortcut for each is Shift + Space for the current row or Ctrl + Space for the column.

2. Select Ctrl + Shift + Arrow Down (or right) to take it all the way to the bottom of your sheet.

3. Right-click on it, and then choose Delete. Be careful not to only press the delete button when doing this. This will not have the same effect; all it is going to do is clear the cell's contents.

- Get rid of unnecessary hidden sheets.

If somebody else has given you an Excel file, they could have hidden additional sheets. To lower the file size, unhide all sheets, and then check to see if you need them. If not, delete them.

- Save in binary format (.xlsb).

This is the best way to reduce file size. If you have created an Excel file that has lots of formulas and data, save it in Excel binary format. All VBAs and Macros will be retained, so you won't have to worry about losing functionality. Most files will reduce by 50%, but it will vary depending on the type of data.

- Get rid of raw data formatting.

Your assignment may require you to present data in a certain way, but if it's not going to be review and is only used for calculation purposes, get rid of the formatting as much as you can.

Be careful when using the Clear Formats option. This will also strip out any currency or date formats from your data which can end up being confusing. Formatting for fonts, borders, and highlighting are all good things to get rid of.

Bypass Workbook_Open

This is often used by people who are still developing their code. The Open event could contain code that will take a long time to run or will configure a project in a way that you don't want it to when you work on the file.

1. Macro security is placed on a trusted document or low.

If you have placed your macro security to "Enable All Macros" or the document has already been set to trusted or it is in a trusted folder, select File, Open, and then choose your file. Hold the shift key down when you select the open button.

Your file may be under the Most Recently Used file. If this is the case, hold the shift key when you select your file from the list.

When you do this, it will prevent Workbook_Open from firing, and it will keep Auto_Open macro from running.

2. Macros security set to prompt.

If you don't have your document in a trusted folder, it hasn't been set to trusted, and the macro security isn't set to enable all macros to run, you can do the same thing as what I listed above.

Normally, opening a document like this, Excel will give you a security bar. However, when you hold the shift key, Excel will give you a window. Since you were holding the shift key when opened the file, you would be able to select "Enable macros," and none of your automacros will run.

Use With… End With

This code will execute a series of statements that will repeatedly refer to one structure or object so that the statement will be used to simply syntax when accessing the members in a structure or object. When you use a structure, you will only read the values of the members, or you will invoke methods and end up getting an error if you trying to assign values to the structure's members used in a *"With… End With"* statement.

"With objectExpression

    [statements]

End With"

The objectExpression is required for the code. This is the expression that evaluates a certain object.

The statements are an option for the code. These are just statements between the With and End With that could refer to the members that are in the object.

End With is required for the code and will terminate the definition of the With block.

When you use this, you will be able to perform several statements on a certain object without having to specify the name of the object several times. This statement block allows you to specify a member of an object beginning with a period, just like the With statement object came before it.

If your code has to access the same object in several different statements, you will find these benefits of using a With statement:

1. You won't have to evaluate complex expressions several times or assign the results to variables that are temporary to refer to the members at different times.

2. Your code will be more readable because it will eliminate repetitive qualifying expressions.

Displaying One Procedure at a Time

This will help you have multiple macros or procedures in one module. Normally, you may find that you code window looks a little like this:

"Sub PrintMySelection()

Dim Copies As Integer

ActiveWorkbook.Worksheets(Array("MyTestSheet", "MyTestSheet2")).PrintOut

Copies = 3

End Sub

Sub SaveCopyofMyWorkbook()

    *ThisWorkbook.SaveCopyAs_*

        Filename:=ThisWorkbook.Path & "\" & _

        Format(Date, "mm-dd-yy") & " " & _

        ThisWorkbook.Name

End Sub"

There are several different procedures in this. Sometimes, this can end up being distracting, so let's look at a quick way to change it so that you can see one macro or procedure at a time.

- Open your Visual Basic Edition by selecting ALT + F11, or you can choose the Developer Tab

- Select through Tools Menu > Options > Editor Tab

- Unselect the tick on the Default to Full Module View checkbox

After that, you can use the drop-down lists at the beginning of your module window to pick the procedure that you want to view or to edit any of the procedures.

Excel VBA Loops

Loops are a basic and important tool in VBA and are pretty much used in any programming language. These are helpful when repeating a block of code until it is provided a condition. Loops enable you to write out a few simple code lines and achieve a greater output through repetition. You have three basic VBA Loops.

- For Loops

    o For... Next Statements

- This repeats a block of code a certain number of times.

> *"For counter_variable = start_value To end_value*
>
> *[code]*
>
> *Next counter_variable"*

    o For Each... Next Statements:

- This repeats a block of code for every object that is in the group. It will repeat execution of the code for every element. The loop will stop when all of the elements in the collection are finished.

> *"For Each object_variable In group_object_variable*
>
> *[code]*
>
> *Next object_variable"*

- Do While Loop

    o Do While... Loop Statements:

- These statements repeat a block of code indefinitely while it continues to meet the specified condition and evaluate to True, and it will stop once the condition turns False. Do While… Loops will test the condition from the start. Since it tests at the start, the loop may not run if the condition isn't met.

"Do While [condition]

[code]

Loop"

   o   Do… Loop While Statements:

- This difference with this statement is that it tests the conditions at the end. The loop will run at least once when tested at the end.

"Do

[code]

Loop While [condition]"

- Do Until Loop

   o   Do Until… Loop Statements:

- These statements will repeat the block of code until a condition is met and evaluates to True. The condition will either be tested at the start or finish of the code. Do Until… Loop is tested at the start and may not run if conditions aren't met.

"Do Until [Condition]

[code]

Loop"

o   Do… Loop Until Statements:

- Like before, this will test the conditions at the end of the code. That means the loop will be run at least once.

"Do

[code]

Loop Until [condition]"

Filter Cells that have Duplicate Text Strings

There will come a time when you want to filter out the cells that contain duplicate text strings. The thing is, this can be difficult if there isn't consistency in the data. Think about this:

- Any text string is able to repeat in a dataset. This could be the name of an area, or city, or anything.

- You are going to see space characters between your words, it's naturally to do so.

- There could thousands of records.

For this, we will look at creating a VBA function to analyze your cells so that they provide you with the TRUE statement if it finds a duplicate word and FALSE statement if it doesn't. You will be able to use this functions just like every other worksheet function used in Excel.

"Function IdDuplicates(rng As Range) As String

Dim StringtoAnalyze As Variant

Dim i As Integer

Dim j As Integer

Const minWordLen As Integer = 4

StringtoAnalyze = Split(UCase(rng.Value), " ")

For i = UBound(StringtoAnalyze) To 0 Step -1

If Len(StringtoAnalyze(i)) < minWordLen Then GoTo SkipA

For j = 0 To i – 1

If StringtoAnalyze(j) = StringtoAnalyze(i) Then

```
IdDuplicates = "TRUE"

GoTo SkipB

End If

Next j

SkipA:

Next i

IdDuplicates = "FALSE"

SkipD:

End Function"
```

After you have come up with your code, you will need to put it into your backend in order for it to work just like any other function.

1. Make sure that you are in the develop tab.

2. Toggle over to the visual basics area. If you want to take a shortcut, ALT + F11 will do the trick.

3. When VB Editor backend opens, you will then right-click onto an object that pulls

4. Head to "Insert" and then choose "Module." Doing this adds the module object for the workbook.

5. Place your code into the code window.

After this has been added in, you will then be able to use this function as a regular worksheet function.

Single Click Selection

While having to select 500 cells or rows in excel may not be hard to do manually, wouldn't it be nice to make it faster?

By using VBA you can do this in one-click. Here's the code:

> *"Sub Select500Cells()*
>
> *Range(Active Cell, ActiveCell.Offset(500, 0)).Select*
>
> *End Sub"*

1. Once you have copied the code, go to the developer tab.

2. Choose visual basic.

3. Once the editor pulls up you will want to right-click on an object.

4. Select Insert, and then choose a module.

5. Insert the code into the module.

6. Close your editor.

It is now a part of your workbook. If you run the code, you will see 500 cells be selected starting from the active cell you have selected. To do this with a single click:

1. Select the customize quick access toolbar.

2. Once that pulls up, make sure that you choose more commands.

3. Once you see the dialogue box, pick "Choose Command From" and then pick macros.

4. Select on the macro that you want to add.

5. Select Add then OK.

Now, all you will have to do is click on the first cell and then on the macro in the QAT.

List of File Names from a Folder

There is an easy way and hard way to do this. We are going to look at the easy way by using a User Defined Function. First, here's the code:

```
"Function GetFileNames(ByVal FolderPath As String) As
Variant

Dim Result As Variant

Dim i As Integer

Dim File As Object

Dim FSO As Object

Dim Folder As Object

Dim Files As Object

Set FSO = CreateObject("Scripting.FileSystemObject")

Set Folder = FSO.GetFolder(FolderPath)

Set Files = Folder.Files

ReDim Results(1 To Files.Count)

i = 1

For Each File In Files

Result(i) = File.Name

i = i + 1

Next File

GetNames = Result

End Function"
```

1. Head to the developer tab.

2. Select visual basic and open the editor

3. Right-click on an object in your workbook and then choose Insert, and then pick Module.

4. Once there, double-click on one of the objects, and then place your code into the window that opens up.

When you are using the function, you can:

1. In any of the cells, add in the folder address where you want to extract the names of the files.

2. Pick a cell that you want the list to be and type in this: *"=IFERROR(INDEX(GetFileNames(cell name),ROW()-2),"")*

3. Copy and paste the formula and you will get your files.

Select Every Third Row

There is no inbuilt function of excel that will allow you to select every third row, but using VBA you can create something that will allow you to do so. This code can also be modified to pick every fifth, sixth, second, or Nth row.

> *"Sub SelectEveryThirdRow()*
>
> *Dim MyRange As Range*
>
> *Dim RowSelect As Range*
>
> *Dim i As Integer*
>
> *Set MyRange = Selection*
>
> *SetRowSelect = MyRange.Rows(3)*
>
> *For i = 3 To MyRange.Rows.Count Step 3*
>
> *Set RowSelect = Union(RowSelect, MyRange.Rows(i))*
>
> *Next i*
>
> *Application.Goto RowSelect*
>
> *End Sub"*

Next, you need to add this to your editor so that you can run it.

1. Head to the developer tab.

2. Select visual basic.

3. While you are in the edit, right-click one of the objects.

4. Select "insert" and then "module."

5. Double-click an object that has been inserted.

6. Add in the code.

7. Close out the editor.

This code can be used in your workbook now.

To change the row number that you want to select, in the code, go through and change all the 3s to 4s and rewrite the first line to say:

"Sub SelectEveryFourthRow()"

Sort Data in Excel Using VBA

There are already different built-in functions to sort data in Excel, but you can come up with a macro to make this as easy as a single click.

When it comes to sorting with VBA, it's important that the Range. Sort method is what gets used when you are writing code. In this, range is talking about the data that you are interested in having sorted. If you want, it is possible for you to come up with a named range instead of using cell references. Using the sort method, there is some important information that you will have provided for different parameters, such as these:

- Key – this is where you will have to specify the column that you want to be sorted.

- Order – this is where you specify if you want the sorting to be descending or ascending.

- Header – this is where you specify if your dataset will have headers or not.

These three are typically enough in most cases; there may be other parameters you need in others.

Sort One Column without Header

Here's the code in ascending order:

> *"Sub Sortnoheaderdata()*
>
> *Range("enter data range").Sort Key1:=Range("cell to start"),*
>
> *Order1:=xlIncreasing, Header:=xlNo*
>
> *End Sub"*

Sort One Column with Header

If your data has some header, you will need to add this information into your code in order for it to be sorted in the second row instead of the first row of data. Here's the code in descending:

"Sub Sortheaderdata()

Rang("enter data range").Sort Key1:=Range("cell to start"),

Order1:=xlDecreasing

End Sub"

Sort Multiple Columns with Headers

Here is the code to allow you to sort several columns at once:

"Sub Sortseveralcolumns()

With ActiveSheet.Sort

    .SortFields.Add Key:=Range("start cell"),

Oder:=xlIncreasing

    .SortFields.Add Key:=Range("end cell"),

Order:=xlIncreasing

    .SetRange Range("start and end cell")

    .Header=xlYes

    .Apply

End With

End Sub"

Sort with Double Header Click

If you want more ease in sorting your data, you can create a code that allows you to double click on a header to sort.

> *"Private Sub Worksheet_BeforeDoubleClick(ByVal Target As Range, Cancel As Boolean)*
>
> *Dim KeyRange As Range*
>
> *Dim Column Count As Integer*
>
> *ColumnCount = Range("DataRange").Columns.Count*
>
> *Cancel = False*
>
> *If Target.Row = 1 And Target.Column <= ColumnCount Then*
>
> *Cancel = True*
>
> *Set KeyRange = Range(Tartget.Address)*
>
> *Range("DataRange").Sort Key1:=KeyRange,*
>
> *Header:=xlYes*
>
> *End If*
>
> *End Sub"*

Whenever one of the headers is double-clicked, the code will then be disabled from its usual functionality.

No matter the code you want to use, you have to add it to your worksheet.

1. On one of your sheet tabs, right-click it.

2. Choose one of the view codes.

3. **Paste** the code that you want to use into the window that your sheet opens up, which houses that data you want to be sorted.

InStr Function

You can use this function to find the position of a specified substring, and it will then return it to its original position it occurred. If you are interested in figuring out the position of the letter "x" in "Excel", if you use this function, you will get a 2.

The InStr function isn't a function of the worksheet; it is only a VBA function. This is just saying that you aren't going to be able to use it in a worksheet.

If you want to find the position of String2, is empty, the function is going to give you the [Start] argument's value.

However, if it is unable to discover the location in the substring in your main string, you will get a 0.

• Discovering the Position From the Start

In this code, you will be looking for the position of the letter "V' in "Excel VBA".

> *"Sub FindFromBeginning()*
>
> *Dim Position As Integer*
>
> *Position = InStr(1, "Excel VBA", "V", vbBinaryCompare)*
>
> *MsgBox Position*
>
> *End Sub"*

Once this is run, you should get the result 7.

- Finding the Position Starting at the Second Word

Let's say you want to find the position of the word "the" in the sentence "The frog jumped and landed in the pond." However, you want it to begin in the second word.

"Sub FindFromSecondWord()

Dim Position As Integer

Position = InStr(4, "The frog jumped and landed in the pond", "the", vbBinaryCompare)

MsgBox Position

End Sub"

When run, you will get 31 in return.

- Finding @ in an Email Address

Use this code:

"Function FindPosition(Ref As Range) As Integer

Dim Position As Integer

Position = InStr(1, Ref, "@")

FindPosition = Position

End Function"

- Highlight Part of a String

The code is as follows:

```
"Sub Bold()

Dim rCell As Range

Dim Char As Integer

For Each rCell In Selection

CharCount = Len(rCell)

Char = InStr(1, rCell, "(")

rCell,Characters(1, Char-1).Font.Bold = True

Next rCell

End Sub"
```

You will find a For Each loop in this code so that it can look through every selected cell. It will look for the position of the opening bracket and uses the InStr function and changes the font of the text that came before the bracket.

Convert Excel to PDF

Before we get started, make sure that when you run these macros, you will get a Save As dialog box where you need to change the save as type to PDF.

1. Print Selection to PDF

This code is going to change the cells that you have selected into a PDF file. If you only click on a single cell, it is smart enough to know you are going to want to convert more than that one cell, so it will ask you to choose a range.

> *"Sub PrintToPDF()"*
>
> *"Dim Rng As Range"*
>
> *"Dim strfile As String"*
>
> *"Dim file As Variant"*
>
> *"If Selection.Count = 1 Then"*
>
> *"Set Rng = Applicaton.InputBox("Select a range", "Get Range", Type:=8)"*
>
> *Else*
>
> *"Set ThisRng = Selection"*
>
> *End If*
>
> *"Strfile = "Selection" & "_"_"*
>
> *"& Format(Now(), "yyyymmdd_hhmmss")_"*
>
> *& ".pft"*
>
> *Strfil = ThisWorkbook.Path & "\" & strfile*
>
> *"Myfile = Application.GetFilename_"*

"(InitialFileName:=strfle,_FileFilter:="PDF Files (.pdf), *.pdf",_Title:="Type in your filename")"*

"If file<>"False" Then save as PDF"

"ThisRng.ExportAsFixedFormat Type:=xlTypePDF,"

"Filename:=_"

"file, Quality:=xlQualityStandard,"

"IncludeDocProperties:=True,_"

"IgnorePrintAreas:=False, OpenAfterPublish:=True"

Else

MsgBox "No File Selected. PDF will not be saved",

vbOKOnly, "No File Selected"

End If

End Sub"

After you pick the range and select OK, it will give you a dialog box where you will then choose where you are going to save the PDF.

2. Print One Table

The will print your chosen table to PDF. When run, you will get a prompt so that you can name the table.

"Sub PrintTableToPDF()

Dim strfile As String

Dim myfile As Variant

Dim strTable As String, r As Range

Applicaton.ScreenUpdating = False

strTable = InputBox("What do you want to name the table?", "Enter Table Name")

If Trim(strTable) = "" Then Exit Sub

"Strfile = strTable & "_"_"

"&Format(Now(), "yyyymmdd_hhmmss")_"

"&".pdf"

"Strfile = ThsiWorkbook.Path & "\"& strfile"

"Myfile = Application.GetSaveAsFilename_"

"(InitialFileName:=strfile,_FileFilter:="PDF   Files(*.pdf), *.pdf",_Title:="Choose a File Name and Folder to Save")"

"If myfile <> "False" Then 'save as PDF"

"Range(strTable).ExportAsFixedFormat Type:=xlTypePDF,"

"Filename:=myfile, Quality:=xlQualityStandard,_"

"IncludeDocProperties:=True, IgnorePrintAreas:=False,"

"OpenAfterPublish:=True"

Else

MsgBox "No File Selected. PDF will not be saved",

vbOKOnly, "No File Selected"

End If

"Application.DisplayAlerts = False"

LetsContinue:

With Application

.ScreenUpdating = True

.DisplayAlerts = True

End With

Exit Sub

End Sub"

Combine Multiple Files into A Single Workbook

Combining multiple files can be done manually, but there is a faster way to do so with a VBA code.

The following code can help you group several Excel workbooks into a specific place into one workbook:

"Sub ConsilidateWorkbook()

"Dim FolderPath As String"

"Dim Filename As String"

"Dim Sheet As Worksheet"

"Application.ScreenUpdating = False"

"FolderPath = Environ("userprofile")&"\Desktop\Test\"

"Filename = Dir(FolderPath & ".xls*")"*

Do While Filename<>""

"Workbooks.Open Filename:=FolderPath & Filename,"

"ReadOnly:=True"

"For Each Sheet In ActiveWorkbook.Sheets"

"Sheet.Copy After:=ThisWorkbook.Sheets(1)"

Next Sheet

"Workbooks(Filename).Close"

"Filename = Dir()"

Loop

Application.ScreenUpdating = True

End Sub"

Doing the following will make the program work for you:

1. Move every single one of the Excel files that you want to group together into a single file on your computer.

2. Open up a new Excel workbook

3. Select ALT + F11. Visual Basic Editor should open.

4. Once the editor opens up, right-click on an object, then choose Insert and then Module.

5. Double click on your module and then add the code into the window.

6. You will need to make a change to your code: *"FolderPath = Environ("userprofile")&"\Desktop\folder name\"*. The part in read needs to be changed to which folder your Excel files are in.

7. Click your cursor anywhere inside of your code, and then select the green button.

The code will then run, and the Excel files will be consolidated into a workbook.

Matrix Falling Numbers Effect

If you have ever watched the movie Matrix, you probably remember the falling code sequence. Let's look at how you can create this in Excel.

1. In the first from A1:AP1, type in random numbers from zero to nine. You can do this manually or use RANDBETWEEN function.

    a. It helps to reduce the column width so that you can see them all on one screen.

2. In A2:Ap32, type in: *=INT(RAND()*10)*

3. Type in this code:

    "Sub MatricNumberRain()

    i = 1

    Do While i<=40

    DoEvents

    Range("AR1"),Value = i

    i = i+1

    Sleep 50

    Loop

    End Sub"

This will add the numbers one to 40 into cell AR1. You will now need to specify three things to give the numbers colors.

1. Choose A2:AP32, select home, then condition, then formatting, and then New Rule.

2. Once there, select "Use a formula to determine which cell to format" and type in: *"=MOD(AR1,15)=MOD(ROW()+A$1,15)"*.

3. Head over to the format, then make sure to change the color of the font to white.

4. Select Okay.

5. Next, in the A2:AP32 range select Home, and then Conditional Formatting, and then Manage Rule.

6. Afterward, in the dialog box, choose New Rule

7. Click on "Use a formula to determine which cells to format" and type in: *"=MOD(AR1,15)=MOD(ROW()+A$1,15)"*

8. Toggle over to the format and then set font color, light green.

9. Select OK.

10. Lastly, in the same range go toggle through to Home, then Conditional Formatting, then Manage Rule.

11. Once you receive a dialogue box, you will then choose New Rule.

12. Click "Use a formula to determine which cells to format" and type in:

    =OR(MOD(AR1,15)=MOD(ROW()+A$1+2,15),MO D($AR$1,15)=MOD(ROW()+A$1+3,15),
    MOD(AR1,15)=MOD(ROW()+A$1+4,15),MOD($A R$1,15)=MOD(ROW()+A$1+5,15))

13. Pull up the format, and switch the color of the font over to green.

14. Select Okay.

Highlight this cell range, and then change its background color to the color black. You will then place in a button or shape and assign it to that particular button or shape.

xlVeryHidden Sheets

If you want to make sure that nobody finds a hidden sheet, xlVeryHidden is for you. In order to use this code, pull up the visual basic environment editor box. Make sure that you change the sheet name to make your worksheet.

Here is the code:

"Sub HideWorkSheet()

Sheets("sheetname").Visible = xlVeryHidden

End Sub"

If you want to unhide the sheet, use this code:

"Sub UnHideWorkSheet()

Sheets("sheetname").Visible – True

End Sub"

Worksheets

Best practices tell us that a range object needs to have a parent worksheet explicitly referenced. A worksheet can be referred to by its .Name property, .CodeName property, or Numerical Index property. A user is able to reorder the worksheet queue by dragging a name tab or you can rename the worksheet by double-clicking on the tab and type in the name of an unprotected workbook.

Let's look at a standard three worksheets. They have each been renamed to Monday, Tuesday, and Wednesday. Let's say that a user comes along and thinks that Monday should be at the end of the queue. Another person comes along and thinks that the names should be in French. Now, your worksheets are names Mardi, Mercredi, and Lundi.

If you used any of the worksheet reference methods, your code is going to be broken.

" 'reference worksheet by.Name

With worksheet("Monday")

> *'operation code here; for example:*

> *.Range(.Cells(2, "A"), .Cells(.Row.Count, "A").End(xlUp)) = 1*

End with

'reference worksheet by ordinal .Index

With worksheets(1)

> *'operation code here; for example:*

> *.Range(.Cells(2, "A"), .Cells(.Row.Count, "A").End(xlUp)) = 1*

End with"

With the changes that were made, the order and worksheet names have been compromised. However, had you used the .CodeName property, the sub procedure would still work.

"with Sheet1

> *'operation code here; for example:*

> *.Range(.Cells(2, "A"), .Cells(.Row.Count, "A").End(xlUp)) = 1*

End with"

The worksheets will be listed by .CodeName, and then their .Name will be in brackets. The order won't change.

Strings with Delimiters Instead of Dynamic Arrays

Here is the generic formula:

"=Trim(MID(SUBSTITUTE(A1,delim,REPT(" ",LEN(A))),(N-1) *LEN(A1) +1,LEN(A1)))"

In order to split the text at a delimiter, meaning pipe, space, comma, and so on, you may use a formula that is based on the LEN, REPT, SUBSTITUTE, MID, and TRIM functions. Here is an example:

"=Trim(MID(SUBSTITUTE($B5,"|",,REPT(" ",LEN($B5))),(C$4) *LEN($B5) +1,LEN($B5)))"

In order to use this, all you have to do is replace a given delimiter with a large number of spaces by using REPT and SUBSTITUTE. You can then use the MID function in order to extract text related to a chose occurrence. The TRIM function is then used to get rid of all of the extra spaces.

Even though the example is created to extract five substrings from column B, you can easily change that to just one.

Double Click Event

By default, shapes within Excel don't have specific ways to handle single and double clicks and contain the "OnAction" property that allows you to handle clicks. However, there can be times where your code will need you to act in a different way on a double click. This subroutine can be added to your project. When you set it to the OnAction routine for the shape, it will allow you to act on double clicks.

```
"Sub ShapeDoubleClick()

        If LastClickObj = "" Then

                LastClickObj = Application.Caller

                LastClickTime = CDbl(Timer)

        Else

                If              CDbl(Timer)              −
        LastClickTime>DOUBLECLICK_WAIT Then

                        LastClickObj = Application.Caller

                        LastClickTime = CDbl(Timer)

                Else

                        If LastClickObj = Application.Caller Then

                                'desired code should be enetered here

                                LastClickObj = ""

                        Else

                                LastClickObj = Application.Caller

                                LastClickTime = Cdbl(Timer)
```

End If

    End If

    End If

    End Sub"

This code will cause the shape to ignore the first click. It will only run your desired code with the second click in the specified timespan.

Open File Dialog

In this, you will create a macro to open up multiple files. You can click on the "Open Multiple files" button in order to run the macro. You will then see the file dialog box open so that you can choose multiple Excel files.

After all of the files have been selected, select OK to open all of them.

```
"Sub opening_multiple_file()

Dim i As Integer

With Application.FileDialog(msoFileDialogFilePicker)

        .AllowMultiSelect = True

        .Filters.Clear

        .Filters.Add "Excel Files", "*.xls*"

        If .Show = True Then

                For i = 1 To .SelectedItems.Count

                        Workbooks.Open .SlectedItems(i)

                Next i

        End If

End With

End Sub"
```

Extract an Email Address

This is going to take you through a function of VBA that will allow for text strings to be an input, and then search through the strings and provide you with the address it initially obtains. The formula will use: *"=ExtractEmailAddress(cell of address)"*.

If the function doesn't find an email adder, the function will give you an empty string. It will only extract the first email it finds.

"Function ExtractEmailAddress(s As String) As String

   Dim AtSignLocation As Long

   Dim i As Long

   Dim TempStr As String

   Const CharList As String = "[A-Za-z0-9._-]"

   AtSignLocation = InStr(s, "@")

   If AtSignLocation = 0 Then

     ExtractEmailAddress = "" 'not found

   Else

     TempStr = ""

     For i = AtSignLocation - 1 To 1 Step -1

       If Mid(s, i, 1) Like CharList Then

         TempStr = Mid(s, i, 1) & TempStr

       Else

Exit For

End If

Next i

If TempStr = "" Then Exit Function

TempStr = TempStr & "@"

For i = AtSignLocation + 1 To Len(s)

If Mid(s, i, 1) Like CharList Then

TempStr = TempStr & Mid(s, i, 1)

Else

Exit For

End If

Next i

End If

If Right(TempStr, 1) = "." Then TempStr = _

Left(TempStr, Len(TempStr) - 1)

ExtractEmailAddress = TempStr

End Function"

Picking Colors that Work

When it comes to picking colors for your worksheet, the World Wide Web Consortium has come up with a formula that will help you to figure out if your colors will be legible:

"Make sure that the foreground and background color combinations will provide a decent contrast when viewed by people who have color deficits or when they are view on a black and white screen."

They believe that:

1. The color brightness different needs to be a number that is located between 0 and 255.

2. The color difference needs to be a number that is located between 0 and 765.

When creating your Excel worksheet, you need to make sure that you pick the right colors and combinations, the color difference should be higher than 500, and the brightness needs to be 125 or higher.

In the end, nobody has ever claimed they can't read a white background and black text. Keep those fancy colors at bay for your column headers.

Determining a Video's Resolution

There are two ways that you are able to figure out the current video resolution.

1. Maximize your Excel window so that you can find the Height and Width properties.

2. Using a function through API.

You will get VBA coding to show you both of these techniques.

This subroutine will maximize the window and will display the height and width.

```
"Sub ShowAppSize()

    Application.WindowState = xlMaximized

    appWidth = Application.Width

    appHeight = Applicaton.Height

    Msg = "Excel's window size is:"

    Msg = Msg & appWidth & "X" & appHeight

    MsgBox Msg

End Sub"
```

The one we've just discussed is an easy subroutine to use and it will only work when used on Excel 5 or later. The main problem with this is that the metric system won't correspond well with pixels. This means that if the resolution is 1024 X 768, the subroutine will tell you it's 774 X 582.

The following subroutine will help you use Window's API function to figure out the resolution.

"Declare Function GetSustemMetrics32 Lib "user32"_

>*Alias "GetSystemMetrics" (ByVal nIndex As Long) As Long*

Public Const Sm_CXSCREEN = 0

Public Const SM_CYSCREEN = 1

Sub DisplayVideoInfo()

>*vidWidth = GetSystemMetrics32(SM_CXSCREEN)*

>*vidHeight = GetSystemMetrics32(SM_CYSCREEN)*

>*Msg = "The current video mode is:"*

>*Msg = Msg & vidWidth & "X" & vidHeight*

>*MsgBox Msg*

End Sub"

Finding Values in a Range or Array

Has there been a time where you were told to only use the unique items that were placed in a certain range? When all of the data has been placed into a database, you will be able to make use of an Advanced Filter function to find all of the unique items. If your data were placed in several different columns, this method doesn't work. Advanced Filter also won't work if the data is in a VBA array.

The following is the syntax for the UniqueItems function *"UniqueItems(ArrayIn, Count)"*.

This first subroutine will generate 100 random numbers and will place them into an array. The array will then be put into the message and function box and will come up with the number of unique integers in your array.

> *"Sub Test1()*
>
> > *Dim z(1 to 100)*
> >
> > *For i=1 to 100*
> >
> > > *Z(i) = Int(Rnd()* 100)*
> >
> > *Next i*
> >
> > *MsgBox UniqueItems(z, True)*
>
> *End Sub"*

This next example will count the number of similar elements that you have in the ranges of the two worksheets. It will make two arrays. The first will have the items in A1:A16 and the second will have the unique items from B1:B16.

```
"Sub Test2()

    Set Range1 = Sheets("name of sheet").Range("A1:A16")

    Set Range2 = Sheets("name of sheet").Range("B1:B16")

    Array1 = UniqueItems(Range1, False)

    Array2 = UniqueItems(Range2, False)

    CommonCount = 0

    For i=LBound(Array1) To UBound(Arry1)

        For j = LBound(Array2) To UBound(Array2)

            If Array1(ii) = Array2(j) Then_

                CommonCount = CommonCount + 1

        Next j

    Next i

    MsgBox CommomCount
End Sub"
```

To practice these examples, here is the code that will help you do so:

```
"Function UniqueItems(ArrayIn, Optional Count As Variant) As
Variant

  Dim Unique() As Variant ' array that holds the unique items

  Dim Element As Variant

  Dim i As Integer

  Dim FoundMatch As Boolean
```

```
If IsMissing(Count) Then Count = True

NumUnique = 0

For Each Element In ArrayIn

    FoundMatch = False

    For i = 1 To NumUnique

        If Element = Unique(i) Then

            FoundMatch = True

            Exit For

        End If

    Next i

AddItem:

    If Not FoundMatch And Not IsEmpty(Element) Then

        NumUnique = NumUnique + 1

        ReDim Preserve Unique(NumUnique)

        Unique(NumUnique) = Element

    End If

    Next Element

    If Count Then UniqueItems = NumUnique Else UniqueItems = Unique

End Function"
```

GetSetting & SaveSetting

Before Excel 97, in order to access the Windows registry, you had to use API calls. After Excel 92, you have two handy functions:

- GetSetting – this finds information in the registry.

- SaveSetting – this will save a setting located in the registry.

Both functions will only work with this key name:

"HKEY_CURRENT_USER\Software\VB and VBA Program Settings"

The following subroutine shows you how these functions work. This will execute once the workbook opens. It will retrieve two pieces of information: how many times you have opened the workbook and the time and date it was last opened.

"Private Sub Workbook_Open()

Dim Counter As Long, LastOpen As String, Msg As String

Counter = GetSetting("XYZ Corp", "Budget", "Count", 0)

LastOpen = GetSetting("XYZ Corp", "Budget", "Opened", "")

Msg = "This file has been opened " & Counter & " times."

Msg = Msg & vbCrLf & "Last opened: " & LastOpen

MsgBox Msg, vbInformation, ThisWorkbook.Name

Counter = Counter + 1

LastOpen = Date & " " & Time

SaveSetting "XYZ Corp", "Budget", "Count", Counter

121

SaveSetting "XYZ Corp", "Budget", "Opened", LastOpen

End Sub"

After this is executed, you will receive a window that will tell you the information that you requested.

Cell Data Type

There will be certain situations where you will have to figure out the kind of data contained within a particular spot. Excel gives you several functions already that will help. These particular functions are ISERROR, ISLOGICAL, and ISTEXT. VBA will also come with functions like IsNumeric, IsDate, and IsEmpty.

The CellType function, which you will get from the VBA code below, will accept a range argument, and then you will receive a string that will describe your cell's data type. The function will return one of the following value, time, date, error, logical, text, and blank.

```
"Function CellType(c)
    Application.Volatile
    Set c = c.Range("A1")
    Select Case True
        Case IsEmpty(c): CellType = "Blank"
        Case Application.IsText(c): CellType = "Text"
        Case Application.IsLogical(c): CellType = "Logical"
        Case Application.IsErr(c): CellType = "Error"
        Case IsDate(c): CellType = "Date"
        Case InStr(1, c.Text, ":") <> 0: CellType = "Time"
        Case IsNumeric(c): CellType = "Value"
    End Select
End Function"
```

In order for this to work in the worksheet, all you have to do is place this code into your module. Then you will be able to enter a formula like:

```
"=CellType(A1)"
```

Common Mistakes

Qualifying References

You need to fully qualify a reference when you refer to individual cells, range, or worksheet.

In this example:

> *"ThisWorkbook.Worksheets("Sheet1").Range(Cells(1, 2), Cells(2, 3)).Copy"*

Nothing is qualified. The references in the cells don't have a worksheet or workbook that is associated with them. If you don't have an explicit reference, Cells will refer to the ActiveSheet automatically. The above code will fail or produce wrong results if there is any other worksheet besides Sheet1 that is the currently ActiveSheet.

The best way to correct this problem is by using With statements.

Type this in:

> *"With ThisWorkbook.Worksheets("Sheet1").Range(.Cells(1, 2), .Cells(2, 3)).Copy*
>
> *End With"*

You can also use a Worksheet variable. This will become your preferred method if you need to reference many different Worksheets, such as copying the information from one sheet to another.

Type this in:

> *"Dim ws1 As Worksheet*
>
> *Set ws1 = ThisWorkbook.Worksheets("Sheet1")*
>
> *Ws1.Range(ws1.Cells(1, 2), ws1.Cells(2, 3)).Copy"*

There is another problem when referencing a Worksheet collection without a qualifying Workbook. For example:

> "Worksheets("Sheets1").Copy

This worksheet isn't fully qualified and doesn't have a workbook. This will fail if you have multiple workbooks referenced in the code. You need to use just one of the following:

> *"ThisWorkbook.Worksheets("Sheet1") '<--ThisWorkbook refers to the workbook containing the running VBA code*
>
> *"Workbooks("Book1").Worksheets("Sheet1") '<--Where Book1 is the workbook that contains Sheet1"*

Never use this:

> *"ActiveWorkbook.Worksheets("Sheet1") '<--Valid, but if another workbook is active the reference will be changed"*

If range objects aren't explicitly qualified, the range refers to the current active sheet:

> *"Range("a1")"*

It is the same as:

> *"ActiveSheet.Range("a1")"*

Deleting Rows or Columns in a Loop

If you have any unneeded fields or records in your data, there is a way to delete columns and rows in Excel by using VBA. You might need to get rid of duplicate rows of data, or you might need to get rid of rows because of a particular problem.

Here is how you can delete rows in Excel:

Type in this code to get rid of row 5.

```
"Sub sbDeleteARow()

Rows(5).Delete

End Sub"
```

If you were to want to get rid of several rows at one time, try this code:

```
"Sub sbDeleteARowMilti()

Rows("5:10").Delete

End Sub"
```

If you need to delete rows because a certain problem, here's how you do it:

The following code will delete the rows between one and ten whose first column contains an even number.

Type in this code:

```
"Sub sbDeleteARowEvenNumbers()

Dim lRow

'Last record number
```

126

```
lRow = 10

'loop from last row until first row

Do While lRow>= 1

'if the cell value is even then delete the row

If Cells(lRow,1) Mod 2 = 0 Then Rows(lRow).Delete

lRow = lRow – 1

Loop

End Sub"
```

Let's see how you can delete columns in Excel. Here is how you can delete a certain column using code:

If you need to delete Column D from your worksheet, type this in:

```
"Sub sbDeleteAColumn()

Columns("D").Delete

End Sub"
```

You can also delete multiple Columns at one time. Here is how you would delete Columns D through F from your worksheet.

Type this in:

```
"Sub sbDeleteAColumnMulti()

Columns("D:F").Delete

End Sub"
```

You can delete a column because of certain conditions.

If you need to delete the first ten columns that have odd numbers in the first row, you need to type in:

> *"Sub sbDeleteOddDataColumns()*
>
> *Dim lCol*
>
> *lCol = 10*
>
> *Do While lCol >= 1*
>
> *'If the cell value is odd the delete column*
>
> *If Cells(1, lCol) Mod 2 <> 0 Then Columns(lCol).Delete*
>
> *lCol = lCol – 1*
>
> *Loop*
>
> *End Sub"*

ActiveWorkbook vs. ThisWorkbook

Sometimes, developers will want to combine two properties into VBA when they are interested in referencing their workbook. ActiveWorkbook is the first, and ThisWorkbook is the second. If you were to be running your code that is housed within the same workbook that you need to work on you won't have this problem to worry about making sure that the things that you are referencing since they will both continue to point to the Workbook. Problems begin to come up when you are working on things that have several Excel Workbooks and when you have to write code for a single Workbook but have to modify or run a different Workbook.

Let's look at the difference between ActiveWorkbook Vs ThisWorkbook.

ActiveWorkbook

This isn't just the workbook you can see as many people think, as you can have many workbook open side by side. The problem is that only one workbook is considered active. The most important thing is to be active. The workbook whose window has been selected is the one that is considered Active.

The workbook that is open in the top window is considered the active one. The property is not going to return information in the clipboard window or the information window is considered active.

When you use ActiveWorkbooks it can get tricky. For practice, try out this code:

"Private Sub Workbook_Open()

MsgBox Iif(Application.ActiveWorkbook Is Nothing, _

"Current Workbook is not Active", _

"Current Workbook is Active")

End Sub"

ThisWorkbook

You will find that it is a lot easier to understand the property of ThisWorkbook because it only has to reference a workbook that your code is using.

ThisWorkbook returns the object that shows a workbook where you are running the macro. You will always have to return the object. Once you have done this a few times, it will become easier for you to do it properly.

Single Document Interface VS Multiple Document Interfaces

You need to understand that Microsoft Excel 2013 and later versions use Single Document Interface, while Excel 2010 and earlier versions use Multiple Document Interface.

This means that people who use Excel 2013 their workbooks will use just one instance of Excel that contains its own ribbon UI.

For Excel 2010 users, every workbook in one instance of Excel uses a common ribbon UI.

This brings up some important issues if you want to integrate a VBA code that will work with the Ribbon.

This procedure must be created to change the ribbon UI controls across every workbook for Excel 2013 and later.

Please note:

1. Every Excel application-level window properties, events, and methods will not be affected. *"Application.ActiveWindow"*, *"Application.Windows"*, etc.

With Excel 2013 and later, all the properties, events, and methods will operate in the top level window. You can retrieve the handle of this by using *"Application.Hwnd"*.

Variable Definition

Let's look at how you can display, initialize, and declare a variable in your Excel VBA. Once the program knows that you are using one, it will be known as declaring a variable. All initializing means is that you will assign the initial value to a specified variable.

The first thing that has to be done before anything else is to append your worksheet with a command button, and then you can put in your codes. Once you've typed them in, click on the command button.

Integer

To store whole numbers, you must use integer variables. Type in:

"Dim x As Integer

x = 6

Range("A1").Value = x"

You should see the number six in the cell A1 after you click the command button. This happens because on the first line of code the variable "x" was declared with the type of integer. After that, you gave "x" the value of six. Then, the system put the "x's" value into the cell of A1.

String

You use these to store text. As an example, use the following code:

"Dim book As String

book = "bible"

Range("A1").Value = book"

132

After you click the command button, you should see the word "bible" in the cell A1. This is how it works:

On the first line of the code, it tells the variable that has the name "book" with the type String. On the next line, we give the "book" the title of "bible". You have to use apostrophes when you initialize String variables. Lastly, when you click the command button, it puts the word bible in cell A1.

Double

This particular variable works more accurately than an Integer, and it will be able to store several numbers after using a common. Type this code:

> *"Dim x As Integer*
>
> *x = 5.5*
>
> *MsgBox "value is" & x"*

You will see a pop-up box that says "value is 6". You just need to click "OK".

Wait, this isn't the right number. We gave it a value of 5.5. Why did we get the number 6? You have to put the variable as Double.

Type this code:

> "Dim x As Double
>
> x = 5.5
>
> MsgBox "value is" & x"

You will get another pop-up box that says "value is 5.5". Now you can successfully click on "OK".

Quick note: longer variables will have larger capacities. You have to use the right type of variables. Because of this, the code will run faster, and errors will be easier to see.

Boolean

You use this variable to hold either the False or True value. Type this code:

"Dim continue As Boolean

continue = True

If continue = True Then MsgBox "Boolean variables are cool"

You will see a pop-up box that says "Boolean variables are cool". You just have to click OK.

Here is how this works: The first line of code gives the variable the name *continue* with the type Boolean. On the next line, you give continue the value of True. Last you use the variable Boolean to display in the MsgBox is the variable will hold True.

Option Explicit

It is strongly recommended that an Option Explicit is used at the start of a code. Whenever this is used, it will end up forcing you to have to declare every single one of the variables.

Put a *"command button"* on your worksheet, and then try this:

> *"Dim myVar As Integer*
>
> *myVar = 10*
>
> *Range("A1").Value = mVar"*

You are not going to get any results when you click on the command button because you misspelled *"myVar"*. Because of this, Excel VBA will place the empty cell's value as an undeclared variable *"mVar"* into the cell A1. When this is used, the above lines will send you an error since nothing was declared with the variable *"mVar"*. You should see an error box pop-up that says: "Compile error: Variable not defined". To remedy this:

1. You need to click "OK". Then, you will need to click on "Reset" to make the debugger stop.

2. Correct the spelling of *"mVar"* so it read correctly as *"myVar"*.

Now, when you click the command button you should see the number 10 in the A1 cell.

When you use Option Explicit when you begin your code, avoid typing in the name of a variable incorrectly.

You can also instruct Excel VBA to add Option Explicit automatically. Here's how:

135

1. Go to the Visual Basic Editor. You will then choose Tools. Now, find Options and click on it.

2. Find Require Variable Declaration, and check the box beside it.

Quick Note: Option Explicit isn't going to be added to any Excel files that already exist. If you want to use it, you have to type in Option Explicit.

Using .Select / .Activate

Most people don't realize that they don't have to use either ".Activate" or ".Select". They use this because when they use Macro Recorder, they see it being generated. Most of the time it really isn't needed.

There are two main reasons why this is necessary:

1. This can make the workbook repaint the entire screen. When you type in *"Sheets("Sheet1").Activate",* if Sheet 1 isn't the one on screen, Excel has to change it. This will cause Excel to repaint the screen to indicate Sheet 1. This will slow down the macros and is very inefficient.

2. It confuses the user since they are changing the workbook while using it. This will cause some users to think they are being hacked because the screen will look like old 90s movies about computer hacking.

Look at this example:

"Public Sub StopUsingSelectAndActivate()

Dim ws As Worksheet

Set ws = Sheet1

ws.Activate 'unnecessary

Dim target As Range

Set target = Sheet1.Range("A1")

target.Select 'unnecessary

target.Value = "Hi"

End Sub"

137

If you need the user to go to or pick a certain worksheet or cell for some sort of input, you will need to use either *".Activate"* or *".Select"*. You can just get rid of any lines that have these in them. They will do more harm than good.

Application.ScreenUpdating = False

There are a lot of people who can write macros in order to manipulate information in a workbook. Most of the time, these macros will do a lot with this new data like replacing formulas or values, choosing different cells, or taking other actions. What this means is that your Excel screen is going to look like it has gone wild during the time this new macro is running.

You can turn off screen updating during the time the new macro is running to prevent all the distracting flashes and to help it fun faster. The next time you decide to make a new macro, think about adding these lines into your VBA:

"Public Sub MakeCodeFaster()

Application.ScreenUpdating = False

' do some stuff

' Always remember to reset this setting back!

Application.ScreenUpdating = True

End Sub"

You just want to make sure you put the first line near the start of the macro and then another one at the end. By doing this, the macro can do it thing behind the screen without having to stop and update it constantly.

Qualify Your Range References

You might experience a certain bug every now, and then that is a pain to debug. This will happen when the code doesn't completely qualify the range reference.

What does qualify the range reference mean?

When you see a code that looks like *"Range("A1")"*, what worksheet is it referring to?

It refers to the *"ActiveSheet"*. This means it is the worksheet that the viewer is seeing.

This is usually harmless a lot of the times. With time, you might add more features to the code and it will take it longer to process. When other users or even you run this code, and you have to click another worksheet, it will cause some unexpected behavior.

Let's look at this example:

"Public Sub FullyQualifyReferences()

Dim fullRange As Range

Set fillRange = Range("A1:B5")

Dim cell As Range

For Each cell In fillRange

Range(cell.Address) = cell.Address

Application.Wait (Now + TimeValue("0:00:01"))

DoEvents

Next cell

End Sub"

If you use "Range()" without choosing a certain worksheet, Excel just assumes you are referring to the active sheet. You can change this by qualifying your worksheet.

Just change:

"Range(cell.Address) = cell.Address"

To say this:

"Data.Range(cell.Address) = cell.Address"

"Data" in the example above refers to the sheet object. There are numerous ways around this code such as *"fillRange"* that reference the right worksheet; this just shows the point without having to type a lot of code.

Function or Sub is Too Long

If you aren't sure if your function is too long, here's a quick tip to follow. If your function can't fit on the screen without you having to scroll to see it all, it is way too long. Let's take a look at how we can make shorter codes that are easier to manage and read. Most people just concentrate on writing codes that work. It is more important to write code that is concise and clear. Concise and short blocks of code are easier to debug and maintain. This allows you to find any errors faster than with codes that are chaotic and long.

- Wrapping variable declaration: You have to always declare variables at the beginning of the scope. It doesn't matter if it is the scope of module, class, or procedure. VBA lets you merge declarations into one row, and this will make your code short and to the point. You need to use the "Option Explicit" statement if you want others to show errors if the variable wasn't declared. This is the best practice to use. Don't wrap too many declarations so the compiler has to constantly scroll right.

Instead of writing this:

"Dim i As Integer

Dim str As String

Dim dat As Date"

Write this:

"Dim i As Integer, str As String, dat As Date"

- Wrapping lines: You can use *":"* in many cases to put many lines of code onto just one.

Instead of typing this:

> *"i = 10*
>
> *str = "Hello"*
>
> *dat = Now"*

Type this:

> *"i = 10: str = "Hello": dat = Now"*

Typing many rows on just one is useful when you want to define and declare a variable with one line like many do with other programming languages, like:

"Dim i as Integer: i = 10"

- The VBA With Statement: The *"With"* statement will define a scope that is referring to just one object and lets you interact with the property directly without needing to reference it each time. The *"."* Characters can be used to reference a property in a certain object.

Don't type this:

> *"Cells(1, 1).Font.Color = RGB (10, 20, 30)*
>
> *Cells(1, 1).Font.Bold = True*
>
> *Cells(1, 1).Font.Size = 20"*

Type this:

"With Cells(1, 1).Font

.Color = RGB(10, 20, 30)

.Bold = True

.Size = 20

End With"

This won't save lines of code. It will let you remove all the recurring references to the object and ensures that every line references the object.

- Use Iif instead of If-Else if possible: This function can be defined by:

"Iif ([Boolean expression], [return if true], [return if false])"

This function will return either value. It all depends on how the boolean expression gets evaluated. It can replace one *"If-Else"* statement where variables need to be defined. You can also nest many *"Iif"* functions together if you need to in order to replace *"If-ElseIf-Else"* statements.

Don't type this:

"Dim I as Integer, str as String

If i = 10 Then

str = "=10"

Else

str = "<>10"

End If"

Instead, type this:

> *"Dim I as Integer, str as String*
>
> *str = Iif(i = 10, "=10", "<>10")"*

- Reference Named Ranges directly: You can reference Named Ranges directly by using square brackets *"[]"* instead of the Named Range.

Don't type this:

> *"ThisWorkbook.Names("MyNamedRange").RefersToRange.Value = "Hello there!""*

Type this instead:

> *"[MyNamedRange] = "Hello there!"*

- Enclose reusable objects: You might find that you have to use specific variables or sets of these variables in your code many times. It would be best if you enclosed these variables or properties into things like a VBA Type object, VBA Enum, or VBA Class.

We sometimes find variables that are closely related or describe on objects properties. You can see in the below example that the code is completely unreadable:

> *"'So many variables... all describing obviously 3 different vehicles*
>
> *Dim car1Type as String, car1FuelLeft as Double, car1Miles as Long, car1License as String, car1Miles as Long*

Dim car2Type as String, car2 Fuel1Left as Double, car2Miles as Long

Dim car3FuelLeft as Double, car3License as Double, car3Miles as Long

car1Type = "Sedan"

car2Type = "Hatchback"

car3Type = "Sedan"

'...What a mess..."

Let's try it this way:

"Enum CarType

Sedan

Hatchback

SUV

End Enum

Type Car

myType as CarType

myLicense As String

myMiles As Long

myFuel as Double

End Type

146

'...

Dim car1 as Car, car2 as Car, car3 as Car

car1.myType = CarType.Sedan

car2.myType = CarType.Hatchback

car3.myType = CarType.Sedan

'... So much better..."

You can see how the second one is a lot easier to maintain and read. If you can enclose the *"Car properties into the Car Type object and the CarType enumeration into an Enum object",* it looks so much better. It really doesn't look shorter but it will translate into fewer bugs and less clutter. Enclosures are very useful because VBA "Intelisense" will place the values inside the enclosures.

You might think about learning to use VBA Class modules to enclose variables and object methods like procedures and functions.

Getting Stuck Using For/If Code

Some people use so much nesting when writing code that you have to scroll right to see all of it.

If you don't understand what I mean by nesting, look at this:

```
"Public Sub WayTooMuchNesting()

        Dim updateRange As Range

        Set updateRange = Sheet2.Range("B2:B50")

        Dim cell As Range

        For Each cell In updateRange

                If (cell.Value > 1) Then

                        If (cell.Value < 100) Then

                                If (cell.Offset (0,1).Value = "2x Cost")
Then

                                        cell.Value = cell.Value *2

                        Else

                                ' do nothing

                        End If

                End If

        End If

        Next cell

End Sub"
```

There is no way that this is clean code. When you hit three plus levels in nesting, you have just gone way too far.

Here is an easy trick to reduce nesting. You need to invert your *If* condition. As you have the code written now, it will only change the value if there are a lot of *If* statements to pass. You can invert this so you make the *If* statement check for opposites. You can just skip the cell to entirely update it.

You can also use this version of the code, it will do the same thing:

"Public Sub ReducedNesting()

    Dim updateRange As Range

    Set updateRange = Sheet2.Range("B2:B50")

    Dim cell As Range

    For Each cell In updateRange

        If (cell.Value <=1) Then GoTo NextCell

        If (cell.Value >=100) Then GoTo Next Cell

        If (cell.Offset(0, 1).Value <> "2x Cost") Then GoTo NextCell

        *cell.Value = cell.Value * 2*

    NextCell:

        Next cell

    End Sub"

These *If* statements can be combined, but this was to illustrate the point.

Most people don't like using labels, but you need to consider it to make the code cleaner and shorter.

Conclusion

Thank for making it through to the end of *Excel VBA*. Let's hope it was informative and able to provide you with all of the tools you need to achieve your goals—whatever they may be.

When you start another project using Excel VBA, you will be ready for anything. Use the things that you have learned in this book in order to improve the way you use Excel VBA and to make sure that you don't make some mistakes that could easily be avoided.

Finally, if you found this book useful in any way, a review on Amazon is always appreciated!

Excel Macros

A Step-by-Step Guide to Learn and Master Excel Macros

Introduction

Congratulations on purchasing *Excel Macros: A Step-by-Step Guide to Learn and Master Excel Macros*, and thank you for doing so.

Even though Excel comes with hundreds of built-in spreadsheet functions, there are times when you want to customize your functions. There is no better way to do so than to create your own functions using Excel macros.

With Excel macros, you have the ability to add your own macros to the Excel menu function and use them as you would the built-in functions any time. A macro is simply a snippet of computer code written in Excel form using the Visual Basic language.

Have you ever thought about how much time you spend on Excel completing small, repetitive tasks? Whether you have or haven't, you must have realized that frequent tasks such as inserting standard text and formatting take up a lot of time. No matter your level of practice in doing these tasks, the 3-4 minutes you spend daily to insert your company details in all Excel Worksheets before you can send them to your clients adds up every day.

In most cases, investing a lot of time in these small repetitive tasks doesn't produce much value. In fact, these are examples of efforts which have little impact on the overall output. By reading this book, you are going to learn how you can automate those small tasks using one of the most powerful Excel features.

Macro, in general, is a complicated topic. This means that if you want to become a pro in programming, you must be ready to learn and master Visual Basic language. This book will help you get started on becoming an advanced programmer in VBA.

There are plenty of books on this subject on the market, so thanks again for choosing this one! Every effort was made to ensure it is full of as much useful information as possible. Please enjoy!

Chapter 1

Getting Started with Excel Macros

Dear Reader,

The end of this chapter should see you well-informed about the basics of Excel Macros. In addition, you should be able to know what they are and why they are important. Let's get started, shall we?

Defining Excel Macro

Because you are just getting started with Excel Macro, we will not go into too much detail this early on. For now, you should just know that Macro is one of the most popular software among the numerous Windows applications. A lot of these said applications come with the Macro software built-in. In this book, we shall be covering how to use it in Excel.

Excel Macro gives users the ability to carry out numerous operations with just a click of the button or by simply changing the value of a cell. Macro will help you perform your daily tasks in the most efficient and interesting way. When we look at it based on productivity, we can say that it lends itself to productivity because it helps reduce a lot of the repetitive work that are usually done manually. Aside from that, it helps one perform operations faster. In fact, if you have tasks which need to be done frequently, Excel Macro is the best tool for you to use.

Can we say that Macro is a programming language?

At this point, the answer is in the affirmative: macro is not so different from Visual Basic. For the moment, you don't have to worry about the history of this language. Let's jump straight into the reasons why you need Excel Macros to make your work and daily life easier.

Why Create Excel Macro?

Many students find macros as something difficult and daunting. Once you understand and master the basics, however, you will find it to be one of the best software to enhance productivity. Here are a few reasons why you should aim to create Excel Macros.

1. Excel is your home

If you are one of those people who like to master quick tips, perhaps you consider Excel as your home. You should consider having keyboard shortcuts that can help you perform multiple tasks instead of only one. For instance, the delete key will only clear individual cell contents but not the comments and formatting. However, if you choose to apply a macro, it will help you delete all cell contents and formatting.

2. You frequently import text files

If you would like to boost the rate of importing a single text file, macros could be the way to go, allowing you to accomplish such a task in just a few minutes. Note, however, that if you want to import various text files at any one time, the macro will take longer to create.

3. You use an assistant

You might be fast when it comes to preparing a new month's sheet or product sheet with the correct headings, but what if you find a way these tasks could be done at no cost to you in terms of time? There's no need to be a master in VBA to create a macro that can automate different kinds of processes. You can simply use a recorder which will retain your keystrokes and convert them into a macro.

4. You want to safeguard information

One great thing about Excel is that it provides security for your formulas, files, and sheets. However, when you want to remove and reapply that security, it might take some time. A macro is the best remedy to use in this case. It will automatically perform the task faster and more accurately.

5. You want to merge information

If you are working with a large dataset and want to combine specific information, it would be tiresome to do it manually. But macros can quickly copy the range into a new data sheet or create an email attachment. The only thing which you must know before using a macro is that data merged by a macro is more advanced.

Recording a Macro

Where is the Excel Macro found in Excel?

If you are a beginner, you may be asking yourself what are "Macro" and "VBA" in the first place. Here is a crucial point: you don't need to worry about those two terms. I will suggest that you view the two terms as the same thing for now.

In this section, we shall be using MS Excel. We will record and write our first macro based on the requirements at hand. Therefore, we begin by explaining how to record a macro.

Macro Recording Basics

When it comes to recording a macro, the first thing to do is to search for the Macro Recorder at the Developer tab. However, in Excel, this tab is hidden, meaning you might not be able to see it quickly. Before you use the VBA macros, the Developer tab has to be accessible. To make the tab accessible, follow the steps below.

1. Select Excel Office Options.

2. An Excel dialog box will show up with options for you to select; pick the option, Customize Ribbon.

3. Check the mark near the Developer in the list box.

4. Finally, click OK and return to Excel.

158

It is important for the Developer tab to be visible in the Excel Ribbon. It will help you start recording a macro by just selecting the option Record Macro on the tab.

Below, we look at the Record Macro dialog box and describe its parts in detail:

Macro Name: It is important that you assign a name to your macro because Excel will give it a default name otherwise. The macro name should describe what it is going to perform.

Shortcut Key: Each macro must have an event that will take place for it to run. This event can include a press of a button or the opening of a Workbook. Once you assign the shortcut key to the macro and you press the key combinations, Excel Macro will start. Note, though, that this field is optional.

Store Macro In: A macro that is stored here means that it has an active Excel file. Therefore, if you open a specific Workbook, you can run the macro.

Description: This field is optional, but it can still be very useful when you have multiple macros in the spreadsheet. In addition, this field allows you to describe the macro to the user in greater detail.

Once the Record Macro dialog box shows up, the steps below will help you create a macro you can use to enter your name into a Worksheet.

1. First, specify the name of your macro. Don't go with the default name.

2. Next, allocate a unique shortcut key, such as Ctrl + Shift + N, to the macro.

3. Select OK and exit the dialog box before you start recording.

4. Click any cell in the Worksheet. Type your name and hit enter.

5. Finally, select Developer —> Code —> Stop Recording.

Reviewing the Macro

Youcan find the macro you created even in a new module. To look at the associated code, activate the Visual Basic Editor. There are two ways to activate the VB Editor.

1. Press Alt + F11.

2. Select Developer —> Code —> Visual Basic.

The project window of the VB Editor has a list of open Workbooks as well as add-ins. This list appears in the form of a tree that one can expand. The previous code you recorded is kept in the module of the available Workbook. Thus, if you double-click the module, the code will show up in the window. The macro should resemble what is shown below:

```
Sub MyName()
'
' MyName Macro
'
' Keyboard Shortcut: Ctrl+Shift+N
'
    ActiveCell.FormulaR1C1 = 'Michael Alexander'
End Sub
```

You could see that the macro we have just recorded is a sub procedure. You should be able to see a few inserted comments by the application; these show up at the top of the procedure. Comments start with an apostrophe, but it is not necessary. We can delete the comments, leaving us with one VBA statement.

Macro Testing

Recall that before we recorded our first macro, we assigned it to the Ctrl + Shift + N combination keys. Now, testing this macro would entail returning to Excel. To do so, below are the steps one can follow:

1. Press Alt + F11.

2. Select the button View Microsoft Excel which can be found in the VB Editor toolbar.

Once that is open, activating the Worksheet comes next. This can be performed on the Workbook with the VBA module or on a different type of Workbook altogether. Click on a cell and use the command Ctrl + Shift + N. This will instantly enter your name in the cell.

Comparison of Absolute and Relative Macro Recording

So far, you've learned about the basics of Macro Recorder interface. It is now a good time for us to dig deeper and start recording macros in earnest. Before we do, it is important to understand the two models of recording in Excel. The first one is the absolute reference, and the other one is the relative reference.

Macro recording using absolute references

The absolute reference is the default mode for Excel. We refer to a cell reference as absolute if it can't automatically adjust when we paste a formula to a new cell location.

Macro recording using relative references

When talking about relative reference in Excel macros, we refer to how the reference automatically adjusts when it's moved or copied from one cell or column to another. This requires you to be careful in the way you apply active cell choice while you run and record the relative reference macro.

Other macro recording terms

Up to this point, you must be familiar with recording your Excel Macros. We'll now look at some other important terms which you must be aware of before handling macros.

File Extensions

Let's begin discussing the Excel 2007, as this contains unique file extensions for Workbooks that have macros. You will notice that for the 2010 Excel versions, Workbooks have a standard file extension which ends with .xlsx. In other words, .xlsx extensions don't contain macros. Therefore, having a Workbook that contains macro saved with the following extension will be removed automatically. You will receive an Excel warning that macros will be disabled when you save the Workbook as an .xlsx file.

However, if you are not ready to lose your macros, save it as an Excel Macro-Enabled Workbook. The extension .xlsx for Workbooks is considered safe. On the other hand, Workbooks with the .xlsm extension are considered as a potential threat.

Recording a Macro in Excel

Use the steps outlined in this section to record macros in Excel.

Step 1: Open an Excel Workbook.

Step 2: Navigate to the Developer tab.

Step 3: Find the Record Macro button.

Step 4: If you are using Excel 2007 or 2010, you need to go at the bottom of the Excel; look in the left side and find the button shown below, encased in a red rectangle.

163

Step5: Click the Record Macro button found in the previous picture.

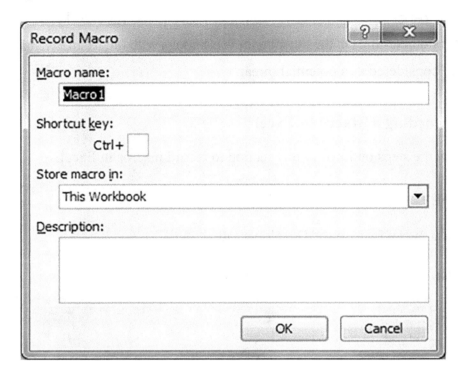

Step 6: If you look at the dialog box shown above, you'll see it has places for you to type the name of the macro. If you want, you can write the name of the shortcut key you would want to use to run the recorded macro. That way, any time you press on that specific macro key, it will run by default.

Step 7: The choice is yours on whether to pick a location to store the macro and/or write a description about the macro.

Step 8: Once you are done filling the fields in the dialog box, click OK and perform a few operations on the Excel sheet. This could include cell formatting or sorting values.

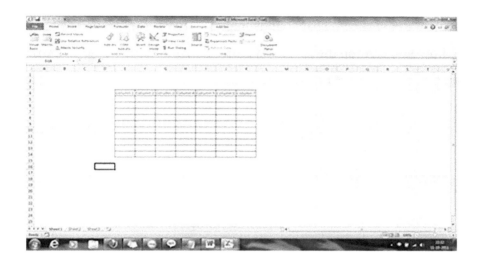

Step 9: If you want to look at your recorded macro, just right-click the sheet name and then go to View Code.

Step 10: Navigate to the left-hand side panel and click it to expand the module.

Step 11: You will see an already created module labeled "Module 1." Click on that module.

Step 12: You will be able to see the code recorded together with the assigned Macro name.

Running the Macro by Pressing the Play Button

There are two ways to run the recorded macro. The first one is by selecting the run button, and the second one is by using the key combination Alt + F8.

In this particular macro, I deleted the formatting done when it was recorded. Therefore, running the macro will make the formatting details show up in the sheet. That sounds magical, doesn't it? Now, it's time to see how you can run the macro by using the run button in the VBA IDE. The image below is of a clean Excel sheet.

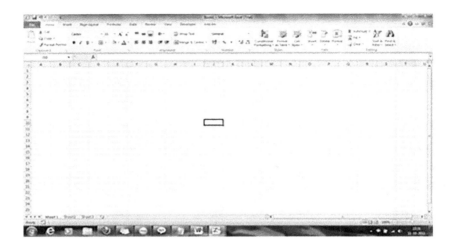

Step 1: Navigate to the screen code that has VBA. The Workbook screen does not display the play button.

Step 2: Hover the mouse's pointer near the particular macro you wish to test.

Step 3: Select the Play or Run button, as indicated by the red box in the following image.

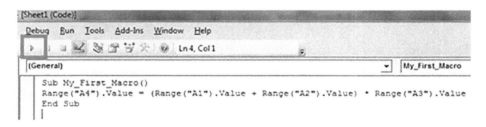

Congratulations on running your first recorded macro! You can look at the image below and compare it with yours.

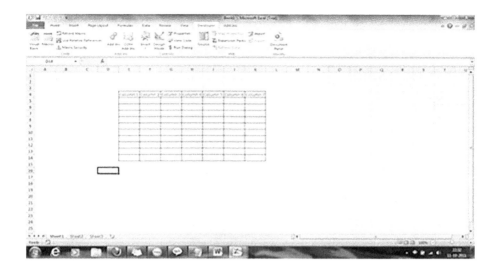

Note

Let's say you failed to position your mouse's cursor around the VBA code that you want to run; the pop-up list below containing all the macros in the Workbook will show up for you to select the correct one.

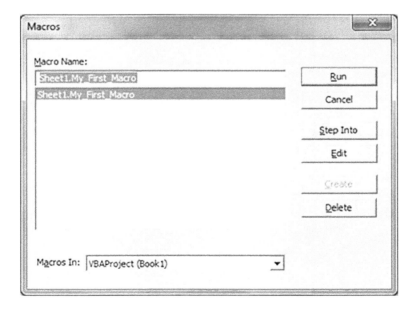

Now that you're getting the hang of things let's find out how you can run the macro without the need to jump to the VBE screen. If you aren't comfortable with the previous method of running the macro, there is another way where you can run it while in the Worksheet screen. Try and use the steps below as well to create and run your macro.

Step 1: Use the Alt + F8 shortcut key. A pop-up screen like the one indicated below will show up.

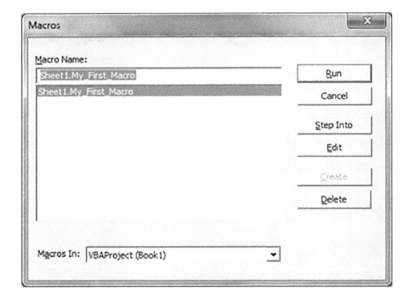

Step 2: A drop-down list will show up; choose your macro.

Step 3: Run the macro by clicking Run.

And you're done! You can now record and play macro in the Excel Workbook.

Chapter 2

Security in Excel Macros

Excel 2010 Macro Security

When Microsoft released Excel 2010, it came with an interesting feature which had new settings on the security model. The most popular update was on the trusted document. This is a document which you have approved to be safe through macros permission.

In Excel 2010, when you open a Workbook which has macros, you will see a yellow message that pops up below the Ribbon to indicate that macros are disabled. Now, clicking on Enable would make it a trusted document. You will no longer be constantly required to enable the content whenever you open the PC.

The concept applied here is simple: once you trust a document through enabling macros, there is no need to enable macros every time you open the document again. This means that Excel records the first time you gave permission and prevents additional messages requesting you to enable the macros the next time you open the Workbook.

This is a great thing because it saves one from the constant annoying messages concerning the macros. No more worries that your macros will fail because macros are disabled!

Trusted Locations

In case you are worried about macros messages showing up, you should decide to create a trusted location. This refers to a specific directory where only trusted workbooks can be considered safe to be kept. This type of location provides one with the use of a macro-enabled Workbook which has no security settings enforced. The only condition is that you must have the Workbook in this location. The steps to create a trusted location are shown below:

1. Choose the Macro Security button located at the Developer tab.

2. Select the button labeled Trusted Location. A Trusted Location menu would appear.

3. Choose the Add New Location button from the list that shows up.

4. Select Browse to look for the directory that you want to consider a trusted location.

Once you have chosen a trusted location, whichever Excel file you open from that location will have macros already enabled.

Storing Macros in the Personal Macro Workbook

A lot of macros created by users are meant to be used on one particular Workbook, but there are some macros that you can use on multiple different works. The Personal Macro Workbook is where these types of macros need to be stored. This means you will always have access to them any time they're needed. This kind of Workbook will be available when you open the Excel program.

To record a macro, it is important that you first select a Personal Macro Workbook in the dialog box. You can find that option in the Macro's drop-down menu. Storing Macros in the Personal Macro Workbook can save time whenever you want to use a Workbook. When you want to exit, a pop-up message will show up to request whether you want to save the changes.

Allocating a Button to a Macro

When you have a macro set up, you need to have an easy and clear way to run each one. A typical button should create an effective and easy user interface. Excel has a set of form controls which could help one create different user interfaces on the spreadsheets. Various types of form controls exist, including buttons and scrollbars.

The basic concept on how to use a form control is straightforward. On the spreadsheet, place the form control in position and assign it a recorded macro. Once you have a macro allocated to a control, you can execute the macro by clicking the control.

Chapter 3

Send Email in Excel Macros

Emails are an important element in any program because they help save the time it would take to go to the email applications. Aside from that, it helps enhance the functionality of the program.

There are a lot of good reasons why you need to automate sending emails inside Microsoft Office Products such as Excel or Word. One reason is that you might want to get a notification when there are updates that happen in the spreadsheets you are working on. You might also need to send a report on the existing data in the spreadsheets.

When you want to be able to send emails from Excel, you need to know some techniques to help you automate the process.

Collaboration Data Objects

This is a messaging component present in Windows and other OS generations. This component already comes with the VBA installation in the Microsoft Excel. This component helps make sending emails in Windows Excel very easy.

Create VBA Macro

The first thing to do is to navigate to the Excel Developer tab, click on Insert, and choose a command button. Move on and create a macro. Once Excel opens the VBA editor, you will be required to add a reference to the CDO library. To do this, go to Tools —> References located in the editor. Go through the list until you can find Microsoft CDO for Windows. Highlight the checkbox before you click OK.

Set Up CDO

At this point, you are good to go and can send emails from Microsoft Excel. To achieve this, create the mail objects and fill all the fields relevant to send the email. Make sure that the TO and FROM fields are filled properly.

Configure CDO to Work with an External SMTP

The next part of the code is to configure CDO to operate with an external SMTP server.

Finalize CDO setup

Once you have connected the SMTP server for sending emails, the next thing to do is to complete all the fields for the CDO_Mail object and specify the Send command. Once you have done this, you will be ready to go. With CDO, you will not see any pop-up boxes like when you are using Outlook Mail object. CDO will combine the email and make use of the SMTP server connection details to trigger the message.

Chapter 4

Beginning Programs with VBA

In this chapter, we are going to learn some basic concepts of programming using VBA.

Data Types, Variables, and Constants

As this text aims to deal with spreadsheet applications, we shall introduce the concept of variables by asking a few questions.

1. What are some of the values that one can enter into a spreadsheet cell?

2. What are the ways you can use these values?

If you have ever used a spreadsheet to manage your data, you are already capable of entering text and numbers into Excel spreadsheet cells. In addition, you might already be capable of changing the format of a spreadsheet cell. Perhaps you can format a number such that the values can show up on the right side of a decimal point, or perhaps you can format numbers so that they appear as a percentage or currency. You might know how to have the texts automatically convert into time or date. Furthermore, you can perhaps change the content of a spreadsheet any time you want.

Typically, cells in a spreadsheet represent a temporary storage location where you can store text and numbers in different formats. This is similar to how a variable is described in any programming language. Variables are used in programming for temporary data storage. This means that the data you enter are converted into variables and are stored as such to later be used in the program.

Declaring variables

Whenever you declare a variable, you make the program reserve a space in its memory to be used later. Variables are declared by using the **Dim** statement. Below is an example:

Dim myClass As Integer

In the above example, the name of the variable is myVar. It is important to note that the name must start with an alphabetic character, but it should not be more than 255 characters nor have spaces. When declaring a variable, avoid the use of unusual characters or punctuation marks when giving it a name. This is because, aside from the underscore character, these are not permitted. The underscore is used to delineate multiple words that exist in a single variable name. When doing variable declaration, avoid using reserved keywords of the VBA language and repeating variable names in the same scope. Make sure that the name of the variable resembles something related to the task it should perform.

Object and Standard Modules

These procedures and declarations come in a set and are all related. Every module contains a separate window in the VBA IDE. In addition, it will contain a separate behavior based on the variable declarations. Modules basically carry all event procedures related to the Worksheet. For object modules, it might have programmer-defined procedures. Every Worksheet will contain a different window code just like the Workbook.

A modularized code is very useful when you want to break complex programming problem into smaller problems and develop a solution for each of them. This process is very important when you want to create software applications.

The Scope of a Variable

When we talk about scope in the context of a variable, we refer to the time when a variable is present in a given section of the program. A variable present in a given scope can not only be accessed but also be further influenced. A variable that is out of scope, on the other hand, is not accessible to the program.

Variables whose declaration falls within a procedural code block is referred to as a procedural level variable. A procedural level program appears only in the presence of program execution inside the procedure where variables were declared. In the figure below, the variable myVar4 is present in the program when we have the Activate () event running on the Worksheet.

When this program execution reaches the End Sub, the variable is cleared from memory. This means it will not be in the scope anymore.

```
Private Sub Worksheet_Activate()
Static myVar4 As Integer
myVar4 = myVar4 + 1
End Sub
```

If you want to make your variable a module level variable, declare it outside the procedure using a Dim statement. The module level variable scope relies on the keyword type that has been applied in the declaration. The keyword declared with these variables include Private, Dim, and Public.

Data Types

The function of data types is to specify the type of value which can be kept in the memory that is set aside for a given variable. Similar to spreadsheet cells, there are many kinds of data types.

Numerical Data Types

Examples of numerical data types include double, integer, long, and single. A variable that has been declared as a long data type or integer can store non-fractional values or whole numbers in a given range. When you want a variable to store a floating point or fractional value, you should apply double or single data types.

Make sure that you check the value assigned to the number. This is because a very big value will cause your program to crash. Again, you should pay attention that you don't mix other data types with numerical data types. This might cause you to fail to get the correct results.

Other Data Types

Other data types include Boolean, Variant, and String.

Constants

In programming languages exists constants. The role of a constant is to help one assign a meaningful name to a string or number, improving the readability of the code. There are a lot of mathematical constants, and that makes it sensible to use the constant data type. You use a constant string in situations that require you to frequently use a given spreadsheet label. We declare constants with the Const keyword. This has been illustrated below:

```
Const PI = 3.14159
Dim circumference As Single
Dim diameter As Single
diameter = 20.34
circumference = PI* diameter
```

You declare and initialize a constant in the same line. What is vital to note is that once we initialize a constant with a value, it remains that way until we change it. This makes it a good move to use a constant in cases where you have to use the same value in the entire program. Constants' names are defined in capital letters.

Using VBA to Input and Output

There are situations that arise while using Excel spreadsheet wherein you require something more dynamic than a spreadsheet cell. In this situation, the easiest way you can collect user input and send the output is through the InputBox () and MsgBox (). The same way Excel has numerous functions that you can use as spreadsheet formulas, VBA has multiple functions designed to help a programmer. In addition, these functions require one or two more parameters so that it can return one or more values.

Gathering User Input with InputBox ()

In case you are faced with a situation where you want to request a user for some input and at the same time prompt a response before program execution proceeds, this is the right function to apply. This function will launch a dialog screen that the user has to address before the execution of a program can resume.

```
InputBox(prompt [,title] [,default] [,xpos] [,ypos] [,helpfile, context])
```

Gathering User Output with MsgBox ()

This function will display a message to the user through a message box. The message box is one of the best ways you can notify the user when a problem happens. It can also be used to throw a question that has a yes/no response to the user. Below is the syntax of a MsgBox ().

179

```
MsgBox(prompt[, buttons] [, title] [, helpfile, context])
```

Manipulating Strings Using VBA Functions

Like most functions, you have to pass at least one or more parameters to the string functions. All these functions should return a value. Below is an example of a syntax:

```
myVar = FunctionName(parameter list)
```

Chapter 5

Procedure and Conditions

This chapter will help you look at procedures and conditions so that you can determine the basic tools that you can work with VBA.

VBA Procedures

We looked at modules in brief in a previous chapter. If you can still recall, we defined it as a set of declarations and procedures that are related. What we didn't say is that a module has its unique window in the VBA code editor. Procedures in programming can be created inside each of the above window modules. Below, we look at various procedures which you can apply in VBA.

Event Procedures

Some of the procedures in VBA include Click () and SelectionChange (). VBA defines the above procedures so that it is not possible to change the existing object or name in the Excel where the procedure is found. In addition, you cannot change the conditions where the procedure is activated. Normally, multiple events are linked with every Excel object in a Workbook or Worksheet. To define event procedures, you need to use the Sub keyword as shown below:

```
Private Sub Worksheet_Activate()
'Event procedure code is listed here.
End Sub
```

In the above figure, the name of the procedure is *Worksheet_Activate ()*
even though most people simply call it Activate (). As you can see in the
above procedure, we haven't passed any parameters to it. This procedure
becomes functional when we activate the Worksheet that it has been
linked to. The procedure ends at the lines End Sub. Still, you can use the
Exit Sub statement in the procedure code to end the procedure.

Parameters that Have Event Procedures

Parameters refer to a collection of variables used by the event
procedures. The parameter values which exist in the event procedure
carry information that is associated with the event. We use a comma to
separate variables as well as declared variable data types. The VBA
language defines all the parameters in the event procedure plus the
number of parameters, data types, and method in which it has been
passed. While you will still be able to make some changes to the variable
names in the parameter list, this is never recommended.

Private, Public, and Procedure Scope

This is not the first time for you to come across the keywords Private
and Public. We use these keywords to define procedures, and they serve
the same purpose as when they are applied to declaring variables. We
use Private and Public to set the scope of a procedure.

As the name suggests, Public keyword allows the procedure to be accessible by other procedures in the project module. On the other hand, the Private keyword is slightly different. This keyword only makes procedures accessible in a given module but prevents its visibility from the rest of other procedures defined. As you can see, it operates the same way a variable scope does. In VBA language, we have Private and Public keywords optional. However, they can be useful in predefined event procedures. In case we remove the Private or Public keyword, the procedure becomes the default.

Tip

When creating general declarations in a module, learn how to apply the Option Private statement so that you can ensure public modules remain visible in the project. If you want to have a reusable procedure, you should remove the Private option.

Sub Procedures

You know that virtually all procedures are subs. Sub is the short form for Subroutine. We use this term to refer to those procedures which have been designed for the programmer's use. A sub procedure's basic declaration is not different from that of an event procedure. This procedure is defined using the Private or Public keywords before it is followed with a Sub keyword, the name of the procedure, and finally the parameter. We end the subprocedures with the statement End Sub. Below is the syntax:

```
Private Sub myProcedure(parameter list)
'Sub procedure code is listed here.
End Sub
```

It is easy to get confused between procedures and sub procedures.
Below, we provide you with how the subprocedure is different:

- Both the variable name and procedure name are defined in the
  parameter list.

- The programmer will decide the number of variables contained
  in the parameter list.

- The process of execution starts when it is called from different
  sections of the program.

- Subprocedures can be placed both in standard and object
  modules.

Tip

When you write procedures, make sure that you aim to keep them short.
You will come to realize that longer procedures become difficult for one
to read, and the same is true when it comes to fixing errors that may
arise. As a general rule, let your procedures remain within a length
where they can be visible in the computer screen.

ByVal and ByRef

These two are keywords used in VBA programming. The ByVal keyword creates a copy of the stored variable. This means that when there is a modification of the created copy, it will not interfere with the original variable.

On the other hand, when we look at ByRef, it is a way for us to pass a variable to another procedure by referencing it. This method of variable passage involves passing the original variable to the procedure. This is not like ByVal where we pass a copy and, therefore, whenever we make any modification to a variable passed by reference, that change becomes permanent.

The most important thing that you need to remember is that we use pass by reference when you want to make some changes to the original variable value. However, in situations where you want to change the variable but still retain the initial value, pass by value is applied.

Function Procedures

These procedures are not different to other procedures apart from just one distinct feature, and that is, they return a value to the procedure that called it. If you have used a few of the basic Excel functions before, then you know how they work. In most cases, we pass one or more values to a function and, in turn, the function must return at least one value.

Creating Personal VBA Functions

To create a function procedure in VBA, use the syntax below:

```
Private/Public Function FunctionName(paramter list) as type
'Function procedure code is listed here
FunctionName = Return value
End Function
```

If you are keen, you should realize that this is similar to the way you define a procedure. It is important that when you create a function procedure, you include Private and Public to specify the scope of the function. The clearest difference is that we have the Function keyword replacing Sub. Furthermore, your function procedure should have a return type. This represents the value which the program will send to the calling procedure. Now, when you fail to define the data type, the return type of the function will be variant.

Tip

Use Exit Function and Exit Sub when you want to switch the program back to the procedure which called it prior to the whole code in the procedure run. Don't forget that we call a function from expressions that would essentially insert a literal or a variable.

186

Chapter 6

Basic Excel Objects

This chapter will talk you through some of the VBA-Excel programming concepts.

VBA Object-Oriented Programming

If it is your first time learning about VBA programming, chances are it's also your first time to hear about object-oriented programming. Don't get scared if this is so. VBA is not an OO programming language. There exist certain features which exclude VBA from being considered an object-oriented programming language, but you will still find some common concepts common to both.

In most cases, VBA and object-oriented language share similarity based on the objects and tools used to change the objects. The tools consist of events, methods, and properties. In other languages, these tools have different names, but they are essentially the same things.

Define Objects

We shall not be abstract in the definition of an object. Essentially, it's the easiest thing for anyone to understand. You should view objects as independent computer programs that have a customized function present for frequent use in programs. The best feature of objects is that they are dynamic; i.e., one can make changes in code.

In the English language, we consider objects as nouns. In programming language, meanwhile, objects can be described using adjectives, and they can carry out different actions (methods). Let's take mathematical shapes as an example. Mathematical shapes can be described by the number of their edges, faces, and their type. We can have a rectangular shape, circular shape, triangular shape, and so on. This means that they all represent the properties of a shape in mathematics.

In short, objects have properties, and we can still associate events with the object. Object events are vital in programming. This is because they provide additional function and interaction between the user and the program. If you really want to know how important object events are, you need to imagine how a program may look if it doesn't have an event. It would really be difficult to achieve a lot of functions without events.

Now, let us review a few objects found in Excel. If you use Excel on a regular basis, you must be familiar with the following: Range objects, Worksheet objects, and Chart objects. Get ready to learn more about these Excel objects and how you can use them.

VBA Collection Objects

This is rather a straightforward thing because these objects are what the name suggests. Collection objects refer to the shape example which we used previously. We can use another example to illustrate it better. Take a vehicle collection—we can have objects of type vehicle in different

188

shapes, sizes, and colors. Rather than a single object, a collection provides the programmer an opportunity to work with objects found in a group.

The VBA language uses the plural form of the object type when referring to a collection of objects. For instance, Workbook object belongs to Workbooks collection object. This collection has all open Workbook objects. The figure below shows two Workbook objects (Book1 and Book3) and three Worksheet objects (Shee1, Sheet2, and Sheet 3).

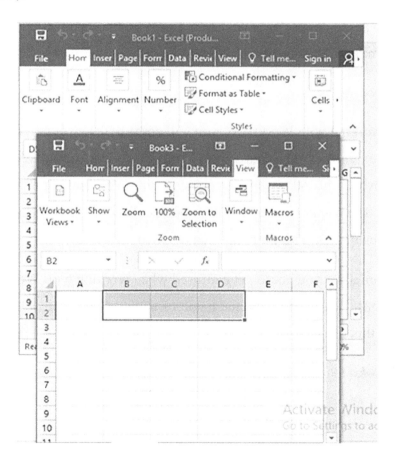

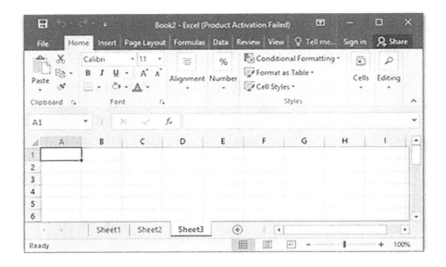

If you want to choose an object from the Workbook collection, use the code similar to the one shown below.

Workbooks(2). Activate

When working with Workbook, you will come to discover that there are two index choices. The first value (1) represents the current Workbook object while the other value represents the Workbook that is being created. The manner in which a Workbook collection object behaves can be confusing, but with time, one can come to master it.

But in order for you not to get confused when working with Workbook, we suggest that if you have the name of a Workbook, you select it by writing this line of code:

*Workbooks(*Book2*). Activate*

Object Browser

The IDE for VBA has a handy way to help one browse through all the existing objects in a project as well as look at the events, methods, and properties. This is referred to as the Object Browser. Use it to determine the Excel model and to know the objects available in the programs. You can also look at all the constants and procedures in the current project.

Select View —> Object Browser to open it, or you can just press F2. Before you begin to use the Object Browser, make sure that you load the library from where you need to look at the required object. Find the Object Model Chart if you wish for a graphical illustration of the Excel object model. But whether you choose to use the Object Model Chart or Object Browser, just remember that we have a hierarchy of objects which one must adhere to. It is essential to look at the object hierarchy as the path that will guide you to the object of interest.

Top-notch Excel Objects

Application object

This comes first in the Excel model. It represents the entire Excel application, and it is a unique object that rarely needs to be used in the code. However, there are a few cases when one may be required to use it: the OnTime () method, for instance, which is used in the program Math Game. Most of the time, you use the Application qualifier to declare features associated with the general appearance of the Excel window. You can view the screenshot below.

```
Application.Width = 600
Application.Height = 450
Application.DisplayFormulaBar = True
```

This object should further be applied together with the ScreenUpdating and WorksheetFunction features.

```
Application.ScreenUpdating = False
Range("A11") = Application.WorksheetFunction.Sum(Range("A1:A10"))
```

However, if you want to define properties of lower-level objects, there is no need to use the Application qualifier.

Workbook and Window Objects

Until this point, you have seen some of the Worksheets and Workbooks collection objects. You know some of the differences between collection objects and regular objects. Another important thing to note is that the Workbook objects rank higher than the Worksheet objects. Those who have used Excel before don't find anything new with this; you know that a single Excel Workbook has several Worksheets.

Not many people can be familiar with the Window objects. Window collection objects existing in the Excel application has all objects open. This includes copies of the Workbook object plus all Workbook objects. The indexing of Window objects is based on the layering.

Worksheet Object

We had previously introduced the Worksheet object, albeit briefly. This belongs to the Workbook object found in the hierarchy of Excel objects. The Worksheet object contains some events related to it. For instance, in a Worksheet's Object module, there exists an event procedure called SelectionChange (). A user entering a value in the current Worksheet would trigger this event.

The Range Object

This is a group of adjacent cells in the Excel Worksheet. In the hierarchy of Excel objects, it is located below the Worksheet object. However, this object is important because it helps one change the properties of a particular cell or a collection of cells in a Worksheet. When writing VBA programs, the range object will become very useful because you will need to use it in most of the Excel applications.

The Cells Property

This property displays a Range object that has one or more column and row indices in the active Worksheet. When you want to return cells back into a Worksheet, use the Cell property in the Worksheet and application objects.

Chapter 7

VBA UserForms and Controls

UserForms denote programmable containers that belong to the ActiveX controls. They allow one to create customized windows which can work as a user interface in the VBA application. They share similar features with VBA objects because they have methods, properties, and events. This chapter will help you understand how you can create UserForms with the help of ActiveX controls.

How to Design Forms in VBA

Those who already have some Visual Basic programming experience understand what UserForms are. For the benefit of the novices: this is basically a form. Since you may not have used VBA forms and this is your first time to interact with this concept, I want you to know that though you might see them as a Window, they aren't quite such. They don't come with a lot of features. For instance, you will not find maximize and minimize buttons. Furthermore, it has few properties and methods to allow one to modify the behavior and appearance of the UserForms object. But all that aside, these forms are still important when you want to improve the user interfaces of your applications.

Forms exist in VBA so that programmers can develop custom user interfaces using their Office applications. Thus far, the only way you know how to enter user data through the dialog box is through the two functions InputBox () and MsgBox (). It is possible to customize forms with the help of ActiveX controls, and it provides more ways for VBA programmers to collect user input.

Add a Form to an Object

If you have your project open and would like to add a form to it, you need to select UserForm from the Menu bar located in the editor. A new folder will show up labeled Forms.

Parts of the UserForm Object

Forms denote different entities in the VBA project. Additionally, each form has its own code that controls it. If you want to check the code related to the UserForm object, click on the icon called View Code from the Project Explorer. You can double-click the form as well or press F7. The general appearance of a code for a form is similar to other modules. In the upper-left corner, it has a dropdown list that has objects in the form. In the upper-right corner, you will find a drop-down list that has all event procedures related to different objects in the form. In addition, there exists a general declaration part used to create declarations of modules in the form.

The UserForm object contains different event procedures. This includes Activate (), Click (), QueryClose (), and many others. A few of these event procedures are common to other ActiveX controls. The figure below shows some of the most common ones.

195

```
SELECTED EVENT PROCEDURES OF THE USERFORM OBJECT

Event              Description
Activate()         Triggered when the UserForm is activated (i.e., shown).
Initialize()       Triggered when the UserForm is loaded.
QueryClose()       Triggered when the UserForm is closed or unloaded.
Terminate()        Triggered when the UserForm is closed or unloaded.
```

The Initialize () event becomes active when we load a form, and it's a wonderful location when the code initializes program controls and variables. The Activate () event is further applied in the initialization, but it is not activated when the UserForm object is loaded.

Adding ActiveX Controls into a Form

UserForm object, like the Worksheet object, resembles a holder that clasps other objects. When we add a form to a project, the Control Toolbox has to automatically show up. If it fails to show up, click View —> Toolbox from the Menu bar.

These form controls exist in a format similar to how they appear when added in a Worksheet. When it is placed in a form, you can access the ActiveX control properties through the Properties window. In addition, you can access the event procedures related to the ActiveX controls through the form module. If you would like to practice using ActiveX controls on forms, go ahead and insert a form to the project after opening your Excel. Modify the Caption property, as well as the properties of the UserForm object.

196

Show and Hide Forms

In Excel, you can display a form by triggering the Show () method. However, when you want to load a form without displaying it in the system memory, use the Load () method of VBA. You can then access all components of the UserForm programmatically once it is loaded in the memory. When you want to hide a form from the user but continue with the program control, the Hide () method is the best to apply. What this method does is to not clear the UserForm object from the system memory. Hence, through the programs, both the form and its details are accessible.

Modal Forms

The Show () method accepts a Boolean parameter which describes whether the form is modal or not. A modal form refers to the one which the user has to address, and it has to be closed before any other part of the Excel application can be accessed. When the form has no mode, the user can choose from any open Window located in the Excel application.

Unless there is a need for user interaction when the form is displayed, modal forms are secure. You can display the form through the Show () method from whichever place in the VBA program. But you must be aware that the way a program might run depends on the point in the procedure where the form has been shown.

Designing Custom Dialog Boxes

Generally, to collect the user input pertinent to the application currently running, forms are used as dialog boxes. The ActiveX controls help one to extend the function of forms from the basic InputBox () and MsgBox () functions.

Scrollbar Control

Most likely, you have used scrollbars in many applications to scroll through long documents. Sometimes, they appear automatically on the bottom or side of the VBA controls to help the user see the whole content. Situations like these don't need any addition; the scrollbars are present to help the user view the entire content. Still, in VBA, there are scrollbar controls which you can apply to the forms in your project to improve the interface. Other user form control includes the Frame control, List Box, and MultiPage Control and many others.

Chapter 8

Derived Data Types in VBA

In this chapter, we introduce derived data types in VBA, namely enumeration, and custom. The custom data types represent a vital data structure which permits one to deal with complex systems that reduce and simplify the code. Enumerated data types are not as complicated as custom data types. Instead, they have a simple data structure which creates codes that are readable.

VBA Custom Data Types

Having a single name, these data types are a collection of related elements of different types. An example is an application that stores and displays customer information found in a database. The database has related information such as age, address, identification number, and name. You may declare five different variables for each of these particular variables, but that would eventually prove to be cumbersome. In fact, the program would end up being longer and less efficient, not to mention difficult to read and difficult to write. Type and End type statements are used to define custom data types. You can see these below:

```
Public Type CustomerInfo
ID As Integer
Name As String * 30
Age As Integer
Gender As String * 1
Address As String * 50
End Type
```

In the example shown above, we have the name CustomerInfo given to a custom data type containing five elements. It is important to make sure that a custom data type definition is done in the general declaration module.

It is also essential that one differentiates between custom data type definition and variable declaration. The variable declaration describes the type of data but not the variable. This means that data is not shown by the custom data type. Therefore, it is okay to assign a public scope to the custom data type.

In the same way, you may want to declare an integer variable to your program's entirety, you may similarly wish to have variables of custom data type in the whole program.

Declaring a variable of type CustomerInfo is not different from a regular variable declaration. In the example below, the declaration results in the creation of a CustomerInfo variable called "customer."

```
Dim customer As CustomerInfo
```

To access individual elements of the custom data type, we use the dot (.) operator. This has been illustrated below:

```
customer.ID = 1234
customer.Name = "Fred Flintstone"
customer.Gender = "M"
customer.Age = 40
```

Other things that one can perform with custom data type include defining elements as arrays, declaring variable arrays, and passing elements of variables to procedures.

Enumerated Types

Enumerated types have several elements, and this data type originates from an integer data type. In this data type, every integer is assigned an identifier. The names of the enumerated types are constants. A constant will allow one to use symbols instead of numbers. This improves the readability of the program.

To define enumerated data types, it is a must to have its elements arranged between Enum and End Enum statements. Below is an example to demonstrate the definition of enumerated data types:

```
Public Enum Weekdays
Sunday = 1
Monday
Tuesday
Wednesday
Thursday
Friday
Saturday
End Enum
```

201

Within the Enum statement, all elements of an enumerated data type are assigned a constant value. The elements can have both positive and negative integers. When there is no exact initialization done, VBA automatically gives the first element the value 0, the other element the value 1, and so forth.

To declare the variables of an enumerated type, we have to use its name. We can assign them any integer value; however, there will be no point of having an enumerated type if we allocate the variable enumerate constant.

Chapter 9

Excel Charts

C harts represent an important tool to help anyone who wants to analyze data and present it in the Excel or spreadsheet application. The only obstacle to creating charts is that it takes longer and that it's steeper compared to other spreadsheet components. You will find this true when you want to program charts in Excel. One of the reasons that explain this difficulty is that the Chart object in Excel is a substantial component. Before you can start to program with the Excel's Chart object, we recommend that you get familiar with the common chart types together with their components.

The Chart Object

We use charts in the spreadsheet applications to interpret data. There are times when the analysis could involve a visual simple inspection of the numerical data that's been charted or even very advanced multidimensional curve.

Advanced data analysis comprises of looking for the parameter minima via the advanced space usually requiring a customized software hosted in a large computer. Thanks to the advancement in technology, this complex analysis can take place in any desktop computer that has Excel application.

When you are building an Excel chart, you can decide to connect the chart into an open Worksheet or a new Worksheet. Creating a chart and storing it in the new Worksheet would leave you with a new entity called a chart sheet. This is unique because its major function is to display the chart. You can't use it to store data.

In addition, the number of charts that can be embedded in a Worksheet is virtually limitless. When you want to use VBA to program chart sheets and embedded charts, you will need to know how to use different objects, and doing so may not be straightforward at first.

Chart Sheets

Earlier, we learned that a collection of Worksheet object belonged to the Worksheets collection objects. A chart sheet doesn't fall into this group because it is not a spreadsheet. However, chart sheets fall into two different object collections. The first is the sheets while the other one is the charts.

The sheets collection has a wide scope that includes chart objects and Worksheet objects. These are different to some extent because Worksheets and chart sheets are two different giants and a collection of objects stores only one category. However, VBA language has a collection of objects which hold only a single chart sheet. That is the Charts collection object.

It is essential to note that Charts collection object presented using a Charts property can only return chart sheets in a given Workbook. If you want to access a specific chart sheet, point out the index using the Charts property. In some cases, it can be difficult to apply the Chart property such that it would show a collection of chart sheets, including the charts that have been embedded in the Workbook itself. An embedded chart is the type of chart arranged on a Worksheet or chart sheet.

Embedded Charts

Accessing embedded charts would call for the application of both ChartObjects and the charts object collection. A ChartObjects collection object has all the ChartObjects in a chart sheet or Worksheet. It is a container which belongs to a distinct Chart object. As you can see, they may look confusing, but with time, you will come to distinguish between the two easily.

Manipulate Charts

There is a high chance that you have problems when it comes to accessing ChartObjects associated with chart sheets. In this section, we dig deep to see how charts can be manipulated, as well as discuss some of the methods one can use to do so.

Create Charts

If you write a VBA procedure which creates a chart, then it is important to make a decision whether you want to create a chart sheet or connect it to the existing Worksheet. The distinction between the two is very small.

Defining a Chart Sheet

The sub-procedure called AddChartSheet () generates a new chart sheet along with specific data from the user Worksheet that are arranged in a column. A dialog box highlights the range of the Worksheet that contains the data. The chart has Add () method, which is useful for creating a column chart in a new chart sheet.

Don't forget that Charts collection objects denote a set of chart sheets contained in a Workbook. Once we add the chart, the existing chart becomes active since it is the only element of the sheet.

Creating an Embedded Chart Sheet

For one to combine an embedded chart into a Worksheet, we have to apply the Add () method of the ChartObjects collection object. Then, we have the AddEmbeddedChart () sub procedure which helps one create a column chart as well as connect the chart to an existing Worksheet called Embedded Charts.

When you want to add an embedded chart, make sure that the Add () method has four parameters to set the position of the Worksheet chart. Don't define the properties of the Chart object if the chart does not have a single series object.

Chart Events

The Chart Object contains different events activated by various activities of the user. A few of these events are quite common, such as

Activate (), MouseUp (), and MouseDown (). However, we have some events which are special to the Chart object.

It is important to know that Chart events aren't automatically triggered with embedded charts even though it is possible to activate Chart objects for embedded charts. The figure below shows available chart events.

CHART OBJECT EVENTS	
Event	Trigger
Calculate	When new or changed data is charted
DragOver	When a range of cells is dragged over a chart
DragPlot	When a range of cells is dragged and dropped on a chart
Resize	When the chart is resized
Select	When a chart element is selected
SeriesChange	When the value of a charted data point changes

Chart Sheets

We enable Chart events using chart sheets. To record the events that are activated by the user in the chart sheet, take the event procedure that can be found in the chart sheet's module and create and combine a different code with it.

If you want to open the window that contains the code, follow the same steps you would apply for a Worksheet. However, it is essential to note that some events which are exclusive to the specific chart may not be applied somewhere else in the chart sheet because there is no means to activate the events. When data is present in a different Worksheet, it is not possible for the user to drag and drop different cell ranges across the chart. Despite that, the remaining chart events will continue to operate as expected.

Chapter 10

Error Handling

Nothing is as important as reading and writing data into the disk drives of the computer in most programming languages. In this chapter, we will look at some of the available tools in VBA which a programmer can use to write code and look at the various tools present in the VBA and Excel.

All computer programs written by developers and programmers contain errors. These errors are referred to as bugs. We say a syntax error has happened when a programmer goes against the rules of a language. The error could be a missing component in a code, a misspelled keyword, or an improper variable declaration. Such occurrences inhibit the program's execution, but it is not difficult to repair syntax errors.

There is another type of error called logic errors. These happen when the code has errors which might lead to the improper functioning of the program. However, logic errors don't cause the same results as syntax errors like preventing program execution. In fact, it's more difficult to spot logic errors. Despite all these, if a programmer abides by the rules of coding and implements correct debugging procedures, there would be limited errors in a program.

In addition to logic and syntax errors, a program's code can produce a runtime error which happens when a wrong input is entered. Some of the examples include the division by zero error or a missing file. Programmers are required to have an additional sense for errors such as this one because if they are not corrected, these errors will prevent a program from running. In short, the program will crash.

Additionally, these types of errors cannot be repaired by changing the program logic. In a situation like this, the program needs other means to handle the error found in the procedures. Whenever the program links with components of the computer and users, the error-handling code has to be present. Validation techniques are a good example of ways to handle error procedures.

The On Error Statement

This statement facilitates error handling in VBA programs. This error has to be followed with instructions for VBA to help set the course of action in case a runtime error happens. The action taken depends on the error type anticipated. This statement has to appear before the code that's expected to produce a runtime fault. The error statement is positioned close to the entry point of the procedure. In situations when an expected error needs the implementation of a unique code block, apply the GoTo statement of the On Error.

Chapter 11

Debugging

When you write programs, you will encounter a lot of problems and struggle to correct some of them. However, it is not easy to detect bugs in a program, and it can be frustrating and strenuous.

Break Mode

When a runtime error happens, a dialog box shows up with the option to click Debug. Once the Debug option has been selected and running, the IDE will also start, displaying the program in the Break Mode. The execution of the program when in this mode remains in the pause state, and one can go through the code line by line to identify factors such as the current values and the order of the code execution. In this mode, you will be able to see the line which generated the error.

If you want to enter Break Mode intentionally, it is important that you specify the points at the required points of the program using a Debug menu item. Breakpoints are also inserted at points where bugs are anticipated to occur when the program is running. This mode happens when the sequence of program execution jumps to the highlighted breakpoint. In this situation, you can choose to reset the program, scan through each line, and continue with the program's operation.

The value that is presently kept in the variable while in the Break Mode can be examined by hovering the pointer of the mouse near the variable name. Logic errors usually happen when a code allocates an incorrect value to a particular variable. With Break Mode, you can identify the errors which may have caused this problem.

There is yet another great debugging technique wherein you step through the code while it is in the Break Mode. You can press F8 if you want to run a single line of code at a time, beginning from the breakpoint. You can verify the execution sequence of the program as well as check the values stored in the variables when the execution of the code occurs line by line.

Immediate Window

Whenever you scan through a code line by line, it can be very stressful and tiresome if you can't get the error quickly. This window offers the ability for one to check program variables, as well as procedures in the standard program execution. To display the Immediate Window, press Ctrl + G when in the IDE. This window always holds a variable and statements to debug a program.

Watch Window

Apart from the Immediate Window, there is another important tool used in debugging VBA programs called the Watch Window. This Window allows one to monitor the value of a variable or expression in the program. While in the Debug menu, you can add Watch to a program expression or else right-click an expression and select the Add Watch option.

Select a specified procedure which you want to watch; it can even be all the procedures. The next thing to be done is to select a specific module that has an expression which you may want to watch, or else choose all the modules. Then, you can choose the type of Watch. This can be a break when we have a change in value. When the program goes into the Break Mode, the selected Watch type will appear in the Watch Window.

Locals Window

This window will show the variable values local to the procedure in the program execution. Make sure that you view this window before you move on to scanning the procedures in the code. This is an important tool when it comes to debugging, as it permits one to see the values of all variables that are local.

Chapter 12

File Input and Output

VBA language has a few objects, functions, and methods which one can use for file input and output. One example for file input and output is the Workbook object alongside its methods to save and open files. In this chapter, we shall discuss the most relevant tools in the VBA language that can be used to the aforementioned end.

When an application in the VBA needs a file I/O, it often requires a limited size of data stored in the variables of the program instead of the Worksheet. Excel gives you the freedom to copy data into a Worksheet so that you can save it in its general form.

File I/O

The Worksheet objects and Workbook have methods to help one open, close, and save an open Workbook in the same way a user can do the same tasks in an Excel application. It is possible to open and save Workbook files by applying different formats in the VBA code.

Opening and Saving Workbooks

The Open () method opens a Workbooks collection object in an Excel file. The figure below shows the syntax for the method, along with all the arguments.

```
Workbooks. Open(Filename, UpdateLinks, ReadOnly, Format, Password, WriteResPassword,
IgnoreReadOnlyRecommended, Origin, Delimiter, Editable, Notify, Converter, AddToMru,
Local, CorruptLoad)
```

It is important to note that you might not be able to use all these arguments. You can learn more about the terms you're unfamiliar with through online resources.

Use VBA File I/O

Besides the methods Open, Save, and SaveAs, there are other object libraries in VBA. Some of the objects are far too complex to be discussed in this chapter.

FileDialog Object

Existing in the Office library, this object is the regular dialog present in all Office applications. The dialog box allows one to precisely define the folder and files used in the program. This object has two methods. The first one is called Show () and the other one is Execute ().

```
DIALOG TYPES USED WITH THE FILE DIALOG OBJECT

Dialog                  Type VBA Constant (FileDialogType)
Open                    msoFileDialogOpen
Save                    msoFileDialogSaveAs
File Picker             msoFileDialogFilePicker
Folder Picker          msoFileDialogFolderPicker
```

The Execute () method allows a user to define an action of the dialog box along with all the files in the Excel application. For instance, the Open dialog box provides the option for the user to select File and open the Execute () method in the FileDialog object.

214

FileSystem Object

This is an object collection method which you can use to define and extract information related to drives, files, and directories.

Open Statement

This statement is applied when reading and writing a data file. The Open statement has different arguments as well as a string which denotes a trail to a particular file. In case the file is not present, one is created. The open statement further needs an access mode and the number of the file.

Random Access Files

With these files, saving the entirety in the memory is not needed; one can simply access specific values within the file. This is achieved by ensuring that individual data elements have equal length before you can write the file.

Conclusion

We want to congratulate you for reading up to the last page. In this book, you have learned how you can create your first Excel Macro. In addition, we have helped you understand the VBA code behind macros. As you might have noticed, to set up an Excel Macro in the Excel recorder is not at all difficult. If your goal is to record a macro and play it, then you are now quite ready to go.

However, if your long-term goal is to become an expert in Excel Macros, it's my hope that this book has created the foundation and the right idea on how to record Excel macros and that it has given you a basic introduction to VBA programming. Besides that, I hope that this book has given you the confidence and motivation necessary to improve your Excel programming abilities.

Don't forget to look for advanced books to read so that you can continue with your journey of becoming an expert in both Excel Macros and VBA programming. Make sure that you immediately begin practicing macros creation, learn the VBA code behind each macro, and try other random things to see what results you get.

If you continue to read more materials and practice Visual Basic for Applications, soon you will be able to gain a better understanding of the whole process and create even more complex and interesting Excel macros.

EXCEL PIVOTTABLES AND DASHBOARD

The Step-By-Step Guide to Learn and Master Excel PivotTables and Dashboard

Introduction

Welcome to the Excel PivotTables and Dashboard mastery guide! This e-book is intended for freelancers who have been asked to implement analyses and consultants who help inform decision-makers. This book will empower you, as the data person, to separate yourself from others in your field by incorporating additional value to your services through making adaptive reports. This book is also both for the Excel aficionado and the intermediate Excel user who wants to get more functionality out of their Microsoft Excel product. Regardless, the goal is to allow you to stay ahead of the other Excel power users with a sleek resource and reference for your skills.

That being said, foremost, this book is a resource for mastering easy, powerful techniques to create, customize, change, and control PivotTables in Excel. As you encounter analysis problems, you may return to this book to help strategize your approach. This book also features some common troubleshooting issues to get you started on solving technical issues.

To begin, let's discuss a quick definition of PivotTables. PivotTables are a collection of built-in tools that Excel uses to compile more comprehensible reports from spreadsheet data, including data from various Excel files. PivotTable tools filter, sort, rearrange, and calculate data to summarize databases.

These PivotTable features allow you to extract specific information into reports, which can facilitate better explorations of trends in data and predictive features. How you extract and extrapolate this data, of course, depends on the purposes of the report. As with any tool PivotTables ultimately only allows you to visualize data in different ways. How these visualizations are interpreted and the conclusions reached depend on the analytical know-how of the analyst.

Expanding the functionality of Excel depends solely on the version of Excel of your client or employer. This includes PivotTables and the functions used within them. Excel 2019 has added more PivotTable features that may not be backwards compatible to an older perpetual license. This is important for freelancers and consultants because these features may not be viewable on the client's native desktop versions of Excel. This lack of backwards compatibility also makes it difficult to recreate and execute newer features on older versions of Excel. Ergo, it is important when conducting your data dissections and compilations on Excel 2019 or Office 365. Reports are always viewable on Microsoft's office live online Excel client.

To begin, let us start with an overview of the purpose and the best uses of this text. The next section will give an exhaustive overview of text features and how to take the best advantage of them.

Overview: Best Use of and Practice

This book is a collection of supplementary information to review before and after the illustrated demonstrations. In addition to being useful for individuals who favor additional instruction and illustration before application, this book is a superior substitute for most online tutorials. Most Excel aficionados became this way through searching for features online. This is a novel and resourceful way to learn; even this book includes the best sources for this purpose as well. However, these online tutorials are scattered and not unified. This book unifies examples and demonstrations.

Note:

Important and noteworthy information will be separated from other texts accordingly. They will be separated from the main text and can occur at any point in the book.

One useful site used to source our demonstration and references is the Microsoft Office Support site. Each demonstration will point to its associated Microsoft Excel exercises for demonstration and practice ("Create a PivotTable to analyze worksheet data," n.d.). This site is useful because it features samples and screenshots from several platforms. These platform versions include Windows (PC), Mac (iOS), and the Microsoft Live web-based platform.

One of the limitations of the Microsoft Office Support site, however, is that the demonstrations do not feature more realistic datasets. The majority of these datasets are simple examples, featuring incredibly small dimensions, i.e. 3x4 datasets with nonsense data within. While these examples serve as a way to clearly demonstrate the functions, they do not demonstrate how the function is actually used to solve problems.

Demonstrations with a Large Dataset

This book will also feature demonstrations using this large, 6370x17 dataset for practice:

http://www3.wabash.edu/econometrics/EconometricsBook/Chapters/Ch03PivotTables/ExcelFiles/EastNorthCentralFTWorkers.xls

This public workbook file was originally crafted for an introductory econometrics course. Specifically, the dataset was created for their chapter covering pivottables ("Introductory Econometrics Chapter 3: Pivot Tables," n.d.). Econometrics itself involves large demographical datasets. PivotTables require continuous data, i.e. data with no empty rows or columns interspersed in between ("Create a PivotTable to analyze worksheet data," n.d.). Therefore, to create this dataset, the census data had to be cleaned and formatted properly for demonstrations. This serves our purpose because it makes a comprehensible yet large enough dataset to demonstrate the power of pivot tables.

For the purpose of our demonstrations, we will be focusing on these specific workbook dataset features:

- Raw "Data" sheet for performing exercises

- Named Ranges for large dataset management

- Summary of stats generated by Excel's Data Analysis add-in

- 6366 individuals with 17 different measured variables

- "Q&A" sheet with simple contextual exercises

This large dataset will be used to demonstrate features on a more complex table, which is closer to what you might be using these features for in the wild. As an effect, you will also be guided through real world troubleshooting and limitations for these functions.

Note:

Demonstration portions are linked to their associated troubleshooting items in chapter 7

Project Flowthrough: Best approach to a project

With an understanding of the main features of the book, we can move on to discussing an overview of topics. This book follows the logical steps from getting started, such as a review of basic functions, to analysis, and the finalization process for a report. The basic flowthrough of the book can be summarized as follows:

(1)Version Considerations and Compatibility

(2) Basic functions

(3) Automation

(4) Analysis

(5) Modeling

(6)Reporting and Sharing

Note:

Instructions on how to navigate the platform will be given in path form. Using the flowthrough process of the book listed above, in path form it would be:

Version Considerations and

CompatibilityBasic functions > Automation >...

...Analysis > Modeling > Reporting and Sharing

With "Reporting and Sharing" being the final step in the instructional path.

Version considerations and compatibility will cover Excel 2019 and Office 365 extensively. It will also overview limitations of previous, "perpetual" licenses. Understanding version considerations and compatibility is important for getting started and for troubleshooting software issues. This book will also discuss meeting and anticipating often "unspoken project requirements" for freelancers. Most of these issues occur in this section, but will be detailed throughout the book in verison considerations.

While this book is intended for both power users and users looking to expand their knowledge of Excel, this book will still review basic functions. Expertise begins with a grasp of fundamentals, and even the savviest expert can learn new basic functions. This section will help you familiarize yourself with the platform. All functions will be labeled for version compatibility.

Basic functions will continue over to the automation and efficiency section. This section will include ways of automating some basic functions in order to establish more efficient workflows. Similar to the previous section, power users may benefit the most from this section, including implementing macros using the Visual Basic (VBA) editor console.

Distinguishing itself from the wealth of tutorials available online, this book will briefly provide an overview of general principals in analysis used to qualify and quantify your data. This book was crafted for the purpose of discussing analysis, which is why the large dataset was selected for the demonstrations. The large dataset uses data pulled from a public source with dynamic values. Demonstrations using this dataset will show you how to identify trends and how to visualize them. Using these raw datasets will make it easier to discuss general principles of analysis. This book will showcase 4 basic analysis techniques to get started.

This book will also discuss modeling features and point to specific Microsoft Support Excel features used to model data. As in previous chapters, some of these features will be Excel 2019 and Office 365 specific. Some features will be backwards compatible and will only be mentioned as a method of modeling in PivotCharts.

Note:

This book will only label Excel 2016 and forward. For Excel 2013 and backwards, please refer to the Microsoft Support Excel Features.

Finally, the last chapter will focus on reporting and sharing This chapter will go into detail about Excel functions and PivotTable features that allow you to transform huge data sets into clear summary reports. As the final step in the process it will encapsulate the previous steps such as modeling and contextual aspects of analysis. This chapter will also go into detail vehicles of sharing your analysis and best practices.

Chapter 1

Version Compatibility

Backward Compatibility

Note:

If you are developing a solution for a client, inquire about your client's version of Excel. Make sure that your sheet will work on their version of Excel; especially so if they are using an older version of Excel.

Google Sheets is a popular product for spreadsheets among entrepreneurs. However, Google Sheets is not fully transferable to Excel.

Backwards compatibility is critical for troubleshooting sheet problems. Backwards compatibility is the ability of a piece of software to interact with previous versions. Microsoft files are backwards compatible, meaning that an *Excel 2013 file* will work on a newer, 2019, Office 365 version of Excel. However, an unmodified 2019 Office 365 file will not be able to work well on a 2013 version of Excel. The Office 365 file will have to be modified to work on the 2013 build of Excel. This can be done through saving the Office 365 file as an 2013 Excel file. This solution can be less than ideal because 2013 Excel files are restricted to only Excel 2013 formulas and features. The majority of the PivotTable features and functions covered in this text are from the latest Excel 2019 build. Therefore, a 2019, Office 365 file with PivotTables and extensive reporting will not be able to work on an Excel 2013 build.

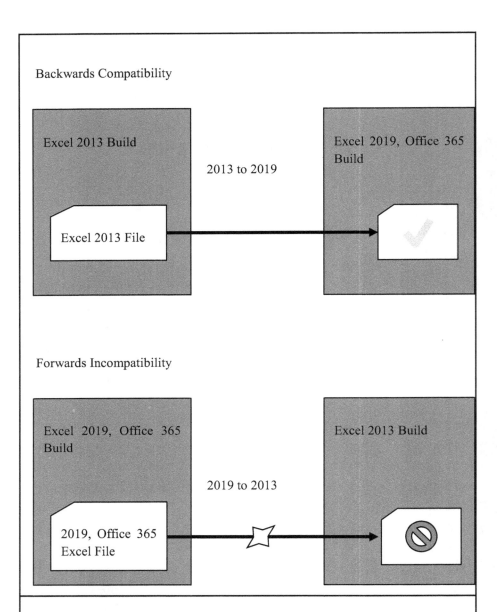

Backwards Compatibility

Excel 2013 Build

2013 to 2019

Excel 2019, Office 365 Build

Excel 2013 File

Forwards Incompatibility

Excel 2019, Office 365 Build

2019 to 2013

Excel 2013 Build

2019, Office 365 Excel File

File Behavior for Microsoft Office Excel: Backwards Compatibility and Forwards Incompatibility

This diagram depicts how different builds of Microsoft Excel builds interact with each other. A "build" is a term that describes a specific version of software. Microsoft practices backwards compatibility, which means that more recent builds will always be able to accept older versions of files. This is illustrated by the top half of the diagram.

However, newer files will not be able to run on older builds. This "Forwards Incompatibility" is depicted by the lower half of the diagram. Microsoft practices forwards incompatibility in order to encourage people still using old builds to update to the latest software for new features.

Note: In Excel, "files" are also known as "workbooks." They are called workbooks because each file can have numerous sheets stored within them. This is a reference to accountants who kept their physical spreadsheets in workbook binders. This distinction becomes important in the automation chapter when you start consolidating different workbooks and sheets. You will need to know the difference in order to instruct Excel properly.

Knowing how backwards compatibility works will inadvertently save you many hours of back and forth. For example, let's say you are a freelancer who developed an Excel sheet that calculates and reports summaries of your client's data. You used your subscription licensed, Office 365 version of Excel.

Your client downloads the sheet to install it into their outfit, but then reports that the product you provided for them is *totally inoperable*. How might you begin troubleshooting? The very first step is to determine what version of Excel your client is using. If you know that your client is trying to use a 2013 copy of Excel, the Office 365 sheet is unable to run on Excel 2013. While you can convert the file to Excel 2013, you may lose the very functionality that the client needed the Excel file to do.

Newer functions are not supported in older software builds of Excel. This forwards incompatibility is embedded into Microsoft's software model as a means to encourage businesses to update to the latest build to take advantage of the newer, and usually more powerful, builds.

Returning to our example, you still may have some options depending on the sorts of features of the sheet. If your client only needs to view the results of reports, you may be able to share the sheet using the Microsoft Live, web platform version of Excel. We'll discuss how to share sheets using the web platform with more specific examples and functionality in later chapters.

How to Check Your Version of Excel

For now, Microsoft has a backward compatibility scheme: newer versions of Excel will always be able to load and render old Excel files, while older versions of Excel cannot handle new Excel file sheets. To begin troubleshooting this issue, you need to check the license of your Excel.

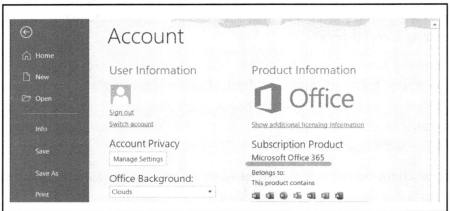

File>Account Screen for Office 365 Excel

The target screen depicting account information. In addition to account information such as the email associated with Microsoft Office Online Live, if you have one, it also shows the current version of your Office products.

For this text, we will be using an Office 365 subscription product. Excel 2019 perpetual license builds will have a slightly different screen.

To access the build and version of your Excel, perform the following steps:

1. Open up a new or existing document to gain access to the main menu

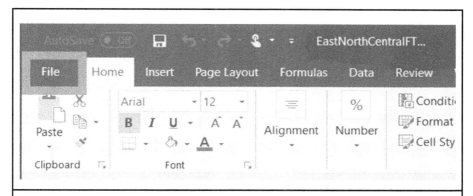

Excel Main Menu

This menu is only accessible when you open up an excel file. This view features the "Home" ribbon that opens as the default upon opening a file.

2. *File > Account*, which produces the "Product Information" page

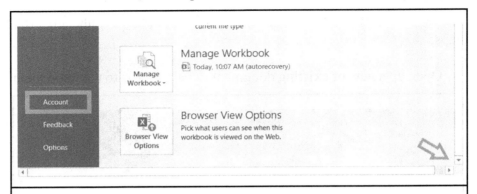

"Account" Location

Be sure to scroll down the Excel: File screen to access the File>Account screen. The Excel: File main screen was designed to be an aggregate of information. There is a lot of information here about the file and other files on your computer in some cases. You will have to scroll down and navigate through to find the items you need.

Note:

You can use "*File > Account*..." on Excel 2016 and later.

Please remember that *only* 2016 and forward build functions and features will be labeled. While this book may discuss features from 2013, they will not be labeled accordingly since they will work on all modern builds of Excel.

The "Product Information" page allows you to see the license, who the license belongs to, and the current version.

Licensing: Subscription versus Perpetual

Microsoft has two licensing schemes: subscription and perpetual licenses. Due to the nature of perpetual licenses, if you have one, you will constantly have to check your copy of Excel and compare it to the latest Excel. Perpetual licenses, as the name suggests, is software that you own the license to forever. These licenses are sufficient for home and student versions of Microsoft software. These licenses are sometimes included with the purchase of a Microsoft Windows laptop computer. This can be a feasible way to purchase Microsoft Office software as the average lifespan of a PC is around 3 to 5 years (Koble, n.d.).

However, one drawback of a perpetual license is that they do not get updated with new features. This may be fine with software like Microsoft Word or Powerpoint. In contrast to other items in the suite, Microsoft Excel is constantly getting upgraded through suggestions of beta test users ("Microsoft wants you to beta test upcoming Office products and services | Windows Central," n.d.). Power users and beta testers will then purchase a subscription-based license. A subscription-based license means that your product will be upgraded with every new release. Microsoft offers its subscription software in a software suite marketed as "Office 365". In the year that this text is composed, both Office 365 and Excel 2019 have the same features. The only difference between them in the current year is that the Excel 2019 refers to a 2019 build under a perpetual license. This current build will be referred to as the Excel 2019, Office 365 build.

Independently, Office 365 requires that you must pay a yearly fee. Subscriptions can become more expensive than the perpetual licenses since new features are only released every 3 years or so. However, Microsoft manages the software updates for you so that you don't have to update your software every three years. There are also other features offered in the Office 365 subscription license that benefits power users, but this text will only focus on PivotTables and other features that make them a powerful analysis tool.

As mentioned before, old features used in the analysis and demonstrations are backward compatible to the Excel 2019, Office 365 build. These older features are also more friendly to old perpetual licenses. As such, in this text, only newer features will be labeled accordingly.

Note

The Microsoft Office Support site labels older versions from 2013 and forward to help mitigate "forwards incompatibility". However, this is not a concern with an Office 365 subscription.

Chapter 2

Basic PivotTable Functions

When discussing software and how it can help us achieve a result, it is important to know the difference between software features and software functionality. Software features are a list of tasks that the software can do. Excel essentially is an extensive calculator that calculates items in real time cell by cell. It uses various functions to achieve certain things, but these functions are just another feature of the program.

Functionality, however, is how a feature can be utilized to achieve a certain result. We want Excel to produce certain deliverables for us, such as reports on a given data set. Features like pivot tables, functions, and slicers allow us to achieve the goal, but using these features is not the end goal.

Stepping back for a moment, the end goal of this text is to use these features in order to learn them. From this perspective, this makes the concept of "functionality" ubiquitous. In other words, while learning aspects of Excel, it may be difficult to grasp the concept of functionality right away because the end goal is to explore features.

It is important to set this distinction between features versus functionality because it will help you deploy Excel in more savvy ways. An Excel power user is not valuable for their knowledge of Excel features. The power user is valuable because they know how to utilize those features to solve any problem presented to them.

To overcome this instructional obscurity between features and functionality, this book deploys examples with a "theoretical goal". Specifically, each demonstration will detail the situational functionality of the feature through providing an example. In this chapter, we will begin by covering new Excel 2019 formulas can be used in calculating items within the pivot table.

Office 365 Excel 2019 Build Features and Functionality

As previously discussed, specific Office 365 Excel 2019 functions and features are not compatible with older builds due to forwards incompatibility. Ergo, Excel files that use specific Office 365 Excel 2019 features will not be able to run on older builds. These Excel 2019 files can still be viewed on Microsoft Office live online web client. We'll discuss sharing and viewing files in detail in later chapters.

These formula functions are important for calculations within pivot tables. Formulas are functions that are called using the "=" sign that allow you to do calculations and other data manipulations. Each function has a specific syntax, or a programmed configuration where you enter operands for the function to operate on. They can also be used as expressions. Expressions are formulas that test if a given condition is true.

Note:

The Microsoft Office Support site has a living catalogue of functions with their build labeled. As of this writing, they only have Office

365 until 2010 labeled, with no 2019. It can be assumed that Office 365 labeled formulas will eventually be categorized as Excel 2019 once the Office Support website updates. You can view the catalogue at their website.

Here are some examples of new Office 365 Excel 2019 functions:

IFS (Office Excel 2019, Excel for Web)

In the past, to test conditions for several scenarios, you had to write a complicated nested IF formula. This new formula allows you to run several logical tests as well as specify the value of each test if the test is true ("IFS function," n.d.).

Here is the syntax for the $IFS()$ formula:

$$IFS(logical\_test1, value\_if\_true1, [logical\_test2, value\_if\_true2],,...)$$

While this function can take up to 127 arguments, the purpose of the function was to reduce large logical nested formulas. Creating a large IFS train of logical tests defeats this purpose. For responsive sheets where data is constantly changing, a $SWITCH()$ function may be more appropriate.

This function is accompanied by $MINIFS()$, $MAXIFS()$, $SUMIFS()$, $AVERAGEIFS()$, and $COUNTIFS()$. These functions can also be used on Excel's web platform. These are functions that allow you to apply some calculation when some conditions are met, where:

$MINIFS()$: When given several ranges, returns the minimum value among them specified by a multiple expressions

MAXIFS(): When given several ranges, returns the maximum value among them specified by multiple expressions.

SUMIFS(): Function within the math and trig functions that, when given several ranges, returns the sum of values among them specified by multiple expressions.

AVERAGEIFS(): When given several ranges, returns the arithmetic mean among them that meet multiple specified criteria.

COUNTIFS(): When given several ranges, counts each cell that meets multiple specified criteria. This function also uses arguments such as the question mark (?) and the asterisk (*).

For example, consider our large dataset and the function *COUNTIFS()*.

[Demonstration, pivot table count if greater than a certain percentage. Purpose is to identify ways of segmenting the dataset that is more meaningful. Not helpful, for example, to look at people who make more than $150k because there are so few in the dataset.]

Recall our discussion about functionality: using features and functions to achieve a specific result. As we have learned, the takeaway is that the advanced IFS functions applies various calculations on ranges based on multiple expressions. This reduces nested arguments to achieve a specific result. However, the IFS functions are better suited for decision making formulas, i.e. calculate the data in this way when a condition is met. For dynamic sheets that have constantly changing data, utilizing a pivottable with a*SWITCH()* may be more appropriate.

SWITCH (Office Excel 2019, Excel for Web)

In programming, switch functions are used to control the operations of program using a single expression. In Excel, the $SWITCH()$ formula would be used to display a specific result based on the data provided. This is helpful for creating dynamic and adaptable pivottables and reports. Therefore, the $SWITCH()$ function is very useful for automating reports, which we will talk about at length in the next chapter.

Here is the syntax for the $SWITCH()$ formula:

$$SWITCH(expression, value1, result1, [default\ or\ value2, result2],$$

$$...[default\ or\ value3, result3])$$

This function evaluates an expression against a list of values and returns an indicated result ("SWITCH function," n.d.).

Other Office 365 Excel 2019 Functions

The various $IFS()$ functions and $SWITCH()$ add more functionality to Excel for analysis and modeling in particular, allowing you to seamlessly add more automated decision making to your sheets. These functions are the most powerful in pivottables because they allow you to call on and calculate data more seamlessly then in previous Excel builds.

Some other functions introduced in Excel 2019 were designed to make text handling easier. $CONCAT()$ is an updated version of the old $CONCATENATE()$ function. This function has the following syntax:

$$CONCAT(text1, [text2], ...)$$

It allows you to combine strings of text from various ranges, however, it does not include the delimiter. For example the formula:

$$= CONCAT("The", "quick", "brown", "fox",$$
$$"jumped", "over", "the", "lazy", "dog.")$$

Would produce:

Thequickbrownfoxjumpsoverthelazydog.

In previous builds of Excel, in order to handle text, delimiters had to be added manually. Microsoft developed $TEXTJOIN()$ for Excel 2019 to add delimiters more quickly. The syntax for $TEXTJOIN()$ is as follows:

$$TEXTJOIN(delimiter, ignore\_empty, text1, [text2], ...)$$

The *ignore_empty* argument is required and indicates whether or not you want the function to ignore empty cells. This is particularly important when using $TEXTJOIN()$ to join a range of cells. Returning to our previous example, we can make the phrase more readable by indicating a delimiter.

$$= TEXTJOIN("\ ", "TRUE", "The", "quick", "brown", "fox",$$

$$"jumped", "over", "the", "lazy", "dog.")$$

Would produce:

The quick brown fox jumps over the lazy dog.

Returning to our conversation about functionality, these text handling functions are useful for automating labeling in PivotTables. Charts and tables must be labeled accurately. Using $CONCAT()$, or $TEXTJOIN()$ for longer complicated ranges of text, allows you to also automate labeling. We will also discuss best modeling and data reporting practices in later chapters.

Forecasting Functions (Office 365 Excel 2019, 2016)

One powerful feature of excel is using historical data to predict future values. Forecasting functions are used to predict future values ("Forecasting functions (reference)," n.d.). There are several functions that use different algorithms for different applications:

$FORECAST.ETS()$: Function that predicts a single future value given historical data using the AAA version of the Exponential Smoothing (ETS) algorithm.

$FORECAST.ETS.SEASONALITY()$: Function that returns a repetitive pattern Excel detects from a specified time series when given historical data using the ETS algorithm.

$FORECAST.LINEAR()$: Function that predicts a single future value given an independent value and historical data using linear (X,Y) regression. Independent values usually occur in units of time.

$FORECAST.ETS.CONFINT()$: Function that returns a confidence interval for a forecast value at a specified target date given historical data.

$FORECAST.ETS.STAT()$: Function that returns one of eight statistical parameters, metrics, or step sizes given historical data. You can learn more about the statistical parameters available for this function at the Microsoft Office Support website ("FORECAST.ETS.STAT function," n.d.).

This has applications in the financial sector for predicting the sales price of products or consumer trends. These functions can also be used to mathematically investigate confidence level and statistical aspects such as data aggregation step size, how the data collasacques into steps. As of now, these functions seem to only be available to Office 365 subscribers. However, the forecast functions are available in Excel web version.

Generally, all the new Excel 2019 formulas simplify certain computations including tasks that would have required nested functions and text handling. The forecast functions are powerful functions that give you access to data prediction and statistics. However, as we discussed, relying on these new formulas for computations will make it difficult to view in older versions of Excel.

Note:

New formulas can still be viewed in the web version. This can be a work around solution for clients with older, perpetual licenses. However, these formulas can only be edited or manipulated with desktop build of Office 365 Excel 2019.

These functions can be deployed inside of PivotTables to control the content of the widgets. Most PivotTable controls can only be viewed in the web version. To implement the pivottables you need a desktop build of Excel.

Enabling Power Pivot Add-in: New Pivot Table Controls on the Desktop Version

Power pivot is the PivotTable wizard for analysis. It is only available for Office 365 subscription licenses, the 2019 perpetual licenses, and the professional plus perpetual licenses ("Where is Power Pivot?," n.d.). It is only available on Windows. You also need to have these desktop versions to use the wizard, however, it is not enabled by default.

To enable Power Pivot for the first time you must initialize the Power Pivot add-in. To do this you must ("Start the Power Pivot add-in for Excel," n.d.):

Note:

Power Pivot is only available on Windows builds of Excel, including Office 365 subscription products. As of this writing, Mac users do not have access to the Power Pivot add-in.

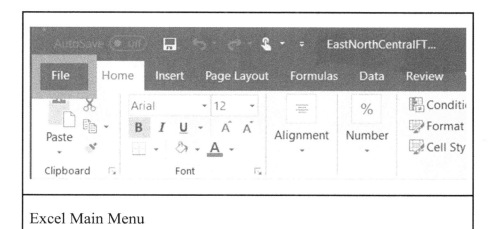

Excel Main Menu

This menu is only accessible when you open up an Excel file.

1. Go to **File** > *Options* > *Add − Ins.*

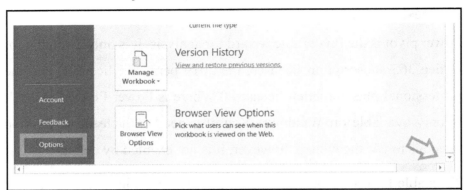

"Options" Location

Be sure to scroll down the Excel: File screen to access the File>Options screen. The Excel: File main screen was designed to be an aggregate of information, therefore, there is a lot of information here about the file and other files on your computer in some cases. This can make it difficult to find the information you need.

You will have to scroll down and navigate to the Options button to access the options window.

2. In the **Managage** box, navigate to $COM\ Add-ins > Go.$

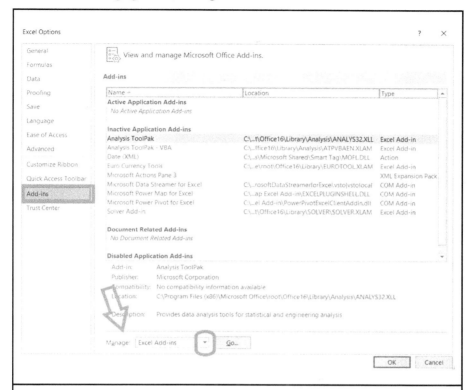

"Add-ins" Dialogue Window

Clicking "Options" will close the Excel: File window and open a separate dialogue window entitled "Excel Options". To access the Excel Options: Add-ins window, you must navigate the menu to the left. The "Manage" box is a drop-down menu at the bottom of the dialogue window. This image shows what appears in the Manage drop-down menu upon opening the window. Click the downward triangle (▼) box to navigate to $COM\ Add-ins$ and click "Go" to access the COM Add-ins dialogue window.

3. Check the Microsoft Office Power Pivot box and click OK.

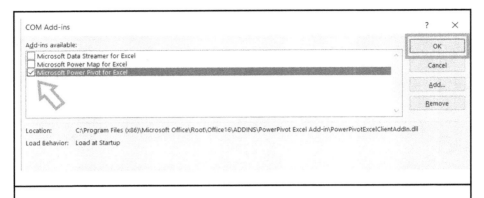

"COM Add-ins" Dialogue Window

Clicking "Go" will close the Excel Options: Add-ins window and open a separate dialogue window entitled "COM Add-ins". Toggle the "Microsoft Office Power Pivot" box and click OK. This will instantly add "Power Pivot" to your main menu ribbon.

Now you will be able to access the Power Pivot add-in from the main menu ribbon:

Excel Main Menu with the Power Pivot Ribbon

Clicking "OK" will close the "COM Add-ins" box and instantly ad the Power Pivot Ribbon. These items are disabled until you generate and select pivottables to manage.

To maintain performance, Excel is programmed to refresh itself if there is a problem with the program. As a result, all Add-ins may disappear.

Specifically, this may cause your Power Pivot ribbon to disappear if Excel closes unexpectedly while the Power Pivot window is opened. Restoring Power Pivot to the menu is covered in the troubleshooting section.

Implementing Your First PivotTable

Looking at the Power Pivot ribbon, you will notice that the features are disabled. You must have at least one PivotTable for it to be activated. For many of the features, you must have several PivotTables to make the most out of Power Pivot features. Let's start with creating and building a PivotTable of average usual hours worked by sex.

1. Select the "Recorded Variables" section of the table

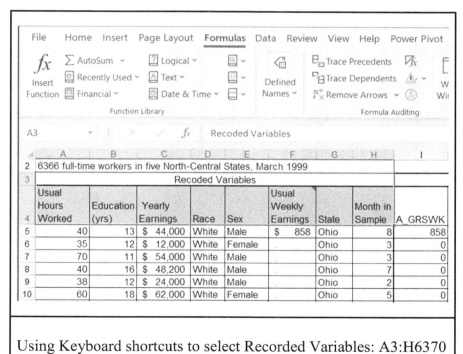

	Usual Hours Worked	Education (yrs)	Yearly Earnings	Race	Sex	Usual Weekly Earnings	State	Month in Sample	A_GRSWK
2	6366 full-time workers in five North-Central States, March 1999								
3				Recoded Variables					
5	40	13	$ 44,000	White	Male	$ 858	Ohio	8	858
6	35	12	$ 12,000	White	Female		Ohio	3	0
7	70	11	$ 54,000	White	Male		Ohio	3	0
8	40	16	$ 48,200	White	Male		Ohio	7	0
9	38	12	$ 24,000	White	Male		Ohio	2	0
10	60	18	$ 62,000	White	Female		Ohio	5	0

Using Keyboard shortcuts to select Recorded Variables: A3:H6370

There are over 6,000 rows. The fastest way to manage a dataset this large is using keyboard shortcuts and the features of the table. Cell A3 spans the section of "Recorded Variables". Select A3, tap the [*Down* − *Arrow*]key, and then press:

[*CTRL*] + [*SHIFT*] + [*END*]

This selects the whole table. To isolate the selection to the Recorded Variables, hold:

[*SHIFT*] + [*Left* − *Arrow*]

It will automatically accept the bounds of Recorded Variables. This saves time in scrolling.

Note:

Creating a named range here is helpful for reducing table scrolling time. A "named range" is a variable you can set in Excel that stands for a range. This sheet already has a "Recorded_Variables" range, but it does not include our target rows and columns. To create a correct range, once you've selected our target range go to:

Formulas > *Defined Names* > "*New*"

A dialogue box will pop up. Name it "Pivot_Table_Values" and it should refer to:

= *Data*! A3: H6370

2. Go to *Insert* > "*Tables*" *drop* − *down* > *PivotTable*

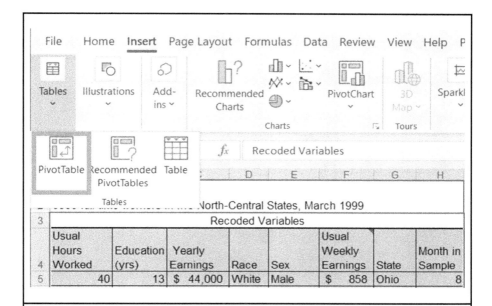

Office 365 Excel 2019 New Layout: Insert>Tables Drop-down Menu

Excel 2019 has a different layout to access PivotTables. This may be jarring to users on older perpetual licenses, or anyone using Microsoft Support Online's general instructions. PivotTables are consolidated with the other tables in a "Tables" section.

3. Create the new PivotTable in Summary Stats

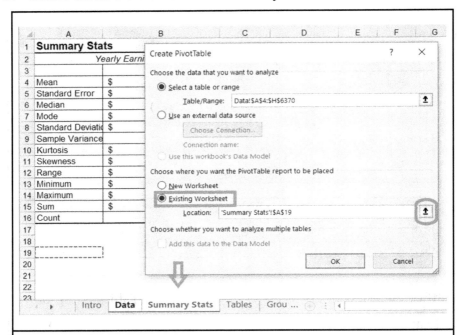

Create PivotTable Dialogue on Summary Stats Sheet

We are placing our first pivottable on the Summary Stats Sheet to in order to keep all of our stats in one place. To access this (1) click on "Existing Worksheet" and (2) in the "Location" box, click the up-arrow icon. This allows you to navigate the workbook. (3) Navigate to the "Summary Stats" sheet and select one of the cells.

If you would like a shortcut, after selecting "Existing Worksheet" you can paste $'Summary\ Stats'!\$A\$19$ into the "Location" box. Hit OK.

4. Build the Pivot Table with the following: Average of Usual Hours Worked and Sex

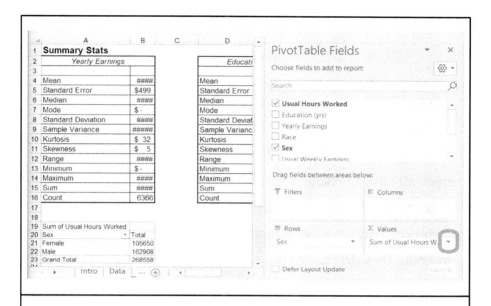

	A	B	C	D	
1	**Summary Stats**				
2	Yearly Earnings			Educati	
3					
4	Mean	####		Mean	
5	Standard Error	$499		Standard Error	
6	Median	####		Median	
7	Mode	$ -		Mode	
8	Standard Deviation	####		Standard Deviat	
9	Sample Variance	#####		Sample Varianc	
10	Kurtosis	$ 32		Kurtosis	
11	Skewness	$ 5		Skewness	
12	Range	####		Range	
13	Minimum	$ -		Minimum	
14	Maximum	####		Maximum	
15	Sum	####		Sum	
16	Count	6366		Count	
17					
18					
19	Sum of Usual Hours Worked				
20	Sex	Total			
21	Female	105650			
22	Male	162908			
23	Grand Total	268558			

Intro | Data

PivotTable Fields

Choose fields to add to report:

Search

- ☑ **Usual Hours Worked**
- ☐ Education (yrs)
- ☐ Yearly Earnings
- ☐ Race
- ☑ **Sex**
- ☐ Usual Weekly Earnings

Drag fields between areas below:

▼ Filters   ‖ Columns

≡ Rows   Σ Values

Sex   ▼   Sum of Usual Hours W. ▼

☐ Defer Layout Update   Update

Create Average of Usual Hours Worked and Sex

After selecting "Usual Hours Worked" and "Sex", Excel automatically populates which value should be in the rows and which should be used for the calculated varaibles. It also automatically populates the pivottable with the calculated sums. However, we want the *Average* *of* *Usual* *Hours* *worked.* To get the Average of Usual Hours worked, click on the down arrow highlighted above and select "Average".

5. Save the current work

Note:

Using $[CTRL] + [S]$ is the safest way to save your work. This is because navigating through the graphical user interface (GUI) features such as the Excel:File window can cause hiccups. This is especially true in resource intensive programs like most Microsoft products, given our experience with the Excel:File interface. Using keyboard shortcuts to save your files reduces computations in the program, thus decreasing the risk of program crashes. To access "Save As" use $[F12]$ or $[fn] + [F12]$ on some newer laptops. This opens a less intensive save-as prompt window.

We will be using this pivottable to demonstrate the Excel 2019 controls in the next chapter.

Control PivotTables Using New PivotTable Defaults

The EastNorthCentralFTWorkers workbook has a Q&A at the end of the book that includes some exercises and demonstrations for the course. These exercises and demonstrations are, of course, specific to the econometrics course. One example is the stark difference between the total average of usual hours worked and the simple average. These are statistic questions that we will not focus on here, but we will create a bar graph showing the demographical data in later chapters.

This chapter will focus on how to manipulate the data on the fly using the pivot table fields. Our first PivotTable entitled "Average of Usual

Hours Worked" only has two variables. Let's begin by creating another, more dynamic pivot table called "Average Yearly Earnings broken down by Sex and Education." The steps will be similar to the previous section.

Building a Pivot Table using Drag and Drop Features

1. Select the "Recorded Variables" section of the table

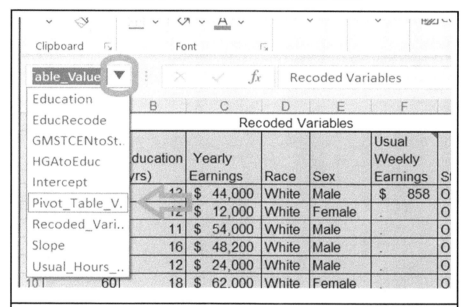

Using Named Ranges in Office 365 Excel 2019

If you named your range "Pivot_Table_Values" in the first demonstration, you should be able to select the range by using this drop down box to the left of the formula bar. Using this drop down bar automatically selects the named range for you.

The down arrow was added in this screenshot to help you with the location of the dropdown. This arrow disappears when the drop-down menu is activated.

2. Go to $Insert > "Tables"\ drop-down > PivotTable$

3. Create the new PivotTable in Summary Stats

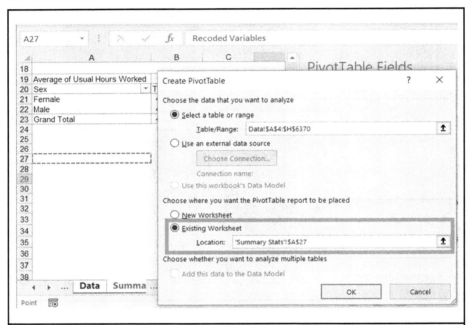

Creating an Additional PivotTable

We will be creating the additional pivottable on the Summary Stats sheet underneath the first one. Click "Existing Worksheet" and copy the following expression into the Location box:

$$'Summary\ Stats'!\ \$A\$27$$

4. Build the Pivot Table with the following: Average Yearly Earnings broken down by Education in the rows and Sex in the columns

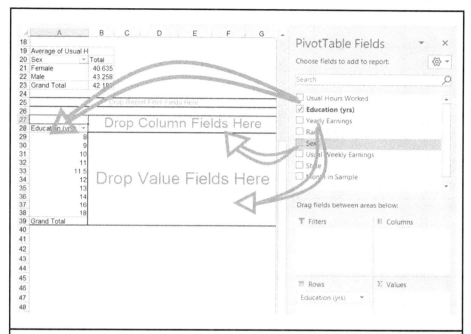

Building a PivotTable using drag-and-drop features

Office 365 Excel 2019 PivotTable defaults allow you to drag and drop fields as well. Click on the field in the list and drag them to the section you want. It is better to start with (1) rows, (2) columns and then (3) values.

5. Be sure to adjust the values to calculate the *average*.

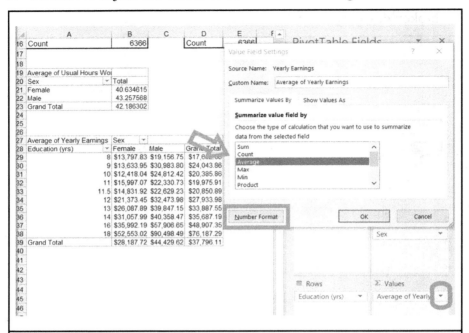

Adjusting the Values

Upon generating the table, Excel automatically calculates the various sums of each category. However, the example asks for the average. Just as before, this can be accessed in the drop down menu underneath values. As this is yearly earnings, this should be formatted as currency. Click on "Number Format" to change the numbers into dollars.

6. Save your progress

this is important for how we structure and clean our data in preparation for pivot table analysis.

Recall that pivottables cannot operate with empty rows or columns. This modified dataset works around this limitation by using the conditional function $IF()$ to fill what would otherwise be 0 in the dataset. These "0" *weekly earnings* entries would mathematically skew the average. It also does not reflect what is happening realistically. These individuals, mathematically and logically, do not receive "0" *weekly earnings*. Replacing it with a string of text, in this case a simple ". "cleans the data of supperiferlous zeros and describes the scenario more accurately. This distinction can also let us hypothesize and compare individuals who report weekly earnings versus those who report only yearly earnings. We could postulate on questions such as, for example, "Do individuals who only report yearly earnings more or less than their peers?" We'll talk more about how we use data for analysis in a later chapter.

	Count of Usual Weekly Earnings	Count Num of Usual Weekly Earnings	Average of Usual Weekly Earnings	Sum of Usual Weekly Earnings
Female	2,600.00	612.00	$577.53	$353,451.00
Male	3,766.00	794.00	$849.81	$674,753.00
Grand Total	6,366.00	1,406.00	$731.30	$1,028,204.00

Target for Pivot Table showing Count, Count Num, Average and Sum for Usual Weekly Earnings broken down by Sex.

The image above depicts the final pivot table for the comparison exercise. You should notice that all of the values have been formatted appropriately. Proper number formatting helps with automation and creating models later on. In the meantime, how might you have the pivottable report on the percentage of individuals reporting weekly earnings in the dataset? Hint: You will need to drag-and drop another instance of "Usual Weekly Reportings" and use the *Value Field Settings > "Show Values As" tab* to calculate.

Excel for the Web: Share your PivotTables with Colleagues

The majority of the value of pivottables is being able to interact with large datasets in various ways. To interact with data you must be on an appropriate platform for data handling, particularly in our case due to the forwards incompatibility of Excel files. Recall our conversation about compatibility. Office 365 Excel 2019 files cannot run on older, perpetual licenses of Excel. This may cause conflict for colleagues or clients using older builds of Excel who want to explore the data. This can be circumvented by using Microsoft's Excel for the web client.

In order to use Excel for the web, you must have a Microsoft live account. If you have a subscription license, OneDrive and all of its sharing capabilities are included in the subscription suite. If you happen to have an Excel 2019 perpetual license, you must have a Microsoft live online account. Once you have an account, follow these steps to host your file onto your Onedrive account:

1. Click the *Share* button in the top left hand corner

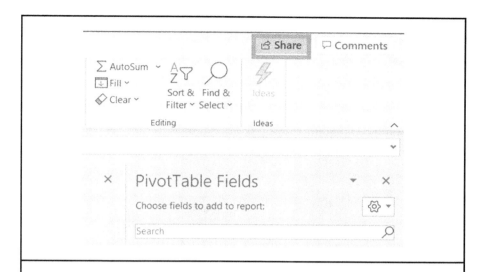

Share Button Location: Top Left Hand of the Excel Main Menu

This is the location of the Share button in Office 365 Excel 2019. This will take you to your OneDrive account. OneDrive is part of the Microsoft Office 365 suite that allows you to store and share your files in the cloud. You do not need a subscription service or even a perpetual license to obtain a OneDrive account. They offer a limited amount of cloud storage for free, enabling you to share and even embed your Microsoft files on the web.

2. If you haven't saved your file to OneDrive, Microsoft will prompt you to save here

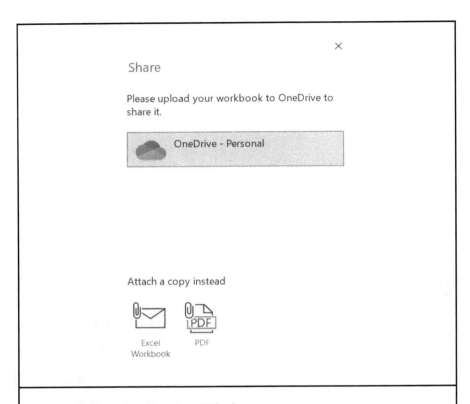

Save to One Drive Prompt Window

In addition to saving and sharing your file on the web, this prompt also gives you options to attach a copy of the file to an email through Outlook or another desktop email client. It is still advised to use Excel for the web, since the web viewer is uniform across operation systems and avoids compatibility issues. Also, pivottables are more valuable as interactive Excel for Web platforms than as static PDFs. Only use PDFs for presentations.

3. To access your file on Excel for the web click "Get a sharing link"

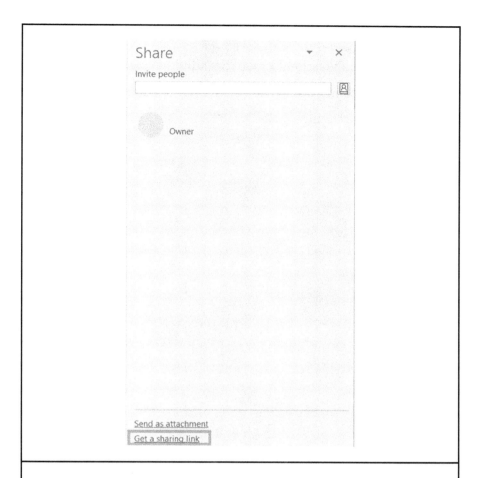

Share Sidebar: Accessing your file on OneDrive

After clicking the Share Button and saving your file to OneDrive, a share sidebar will appear on the left hand side. It will give you the option to attach and send the file. To access your file's OneDrive location, click on the "Get a sharing link" at the bottom of the sidebar.

There are two modes of Excel for the web: viewing, also listed as "Read Only" mode, and editing. Both come with their pros and cons, which we will discuss in the following sections.

Read Only Mode

Read only mode is the default mode for individuals who are not signed-in. You can also send your client Read Only Mode Excel for the Web environments by selecting:

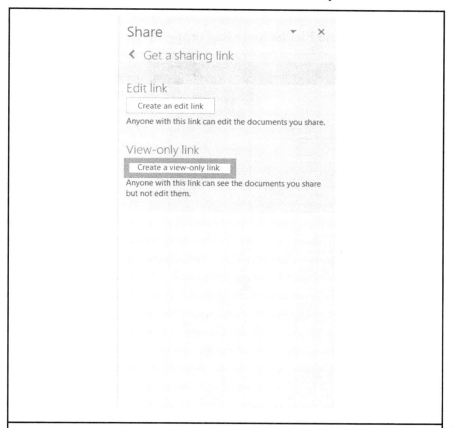

Share Sidebar: Get a Sharing Link, Read Only Mode

It is advised to use Read/View only mode links when possible. Microsoft uses Sharepoint as its backend powering OneDrive. As a result, it's not as flexible with various people making edits to a file from different locations. It can cause file conflicts that result in various instances of a file in the OneDrive. Thus, the workaround is to only share Read-Only files. You have the capability to manipulate pivot tables in Read-Only files.

Using Read-Only mode helps protect the original data of the sheet. Viewers can still manipulate pivot tables by clicking on the pivottable and using PivotTable Fields, including dragging and dropping fields.

Read-Only Mode Demonstration: Drag and Drop

Excel for web in Read-Only mode lets you drag and drop and manipulate PivotTable fields without disrupting the tables. This screenshot depicts a change in our first PivotTable, introducing "Months in Sample" as a filter variable for the pivottable. This view is ideal because clients can manipulative the data without destroying the pivottable structure. At any time, they can reset the pivottable view by refreshing the page.

The PivotTable Fields sidebar is available by toggling the "Field List" button to the left.

Another major benefit of Read-Only mode is that it's automatic for people who do not have a OneDrive account. No sign in is necessary to see this mode, even for people who accidently obtained an editing link. This is for perfect for live presentations where you may have to do simple demonstrations labs of data analysis. This is excellent for consultants who have to explain their work.

Editing Mode

You also have the option of sharing an editing file. This is good for teams who have an aggregate amount of data, especially for adding additional datasets to pivottable analysis. As aforementioned, having files in Editing Mode carries some risk. The sharepoint system can potentially add various files from various sources due to version mismanagement in the system. However, this does help with tracking file versions.

Note:

When sharing editing links, it is always advised to save a seperate file in case of editing mishaps, such as corruption due to a crash. While previous files can be restored from the cloud, it is better to err on the side of caution.

Office 356 Excel 2019 has some features that are not yet supported on Excel for Web. Therefore, after signing in, it will inform you that you must edit a copy of the workbook without the Office 365 Excel 2019 features.

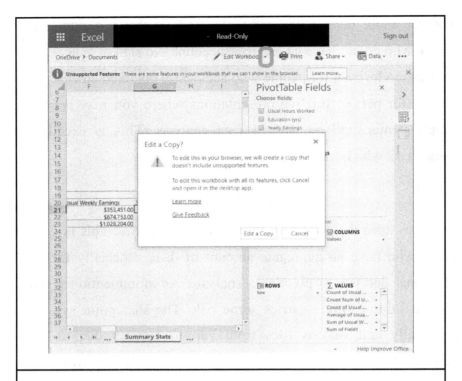

Accessing Editing Mode

Excel for web in Editing mode requires that you sign in to your Microsoft Account. After signing in, clicking the "Edit in Browser" drop-down menu brings you to this prompt, requesting that you edit a copy in Excel for web.

Going to *Edit in Browser drop − down >* *"Open in Desktop App"*gives you the option to open the file locally on your computer in your desktop build of Excel. However, this isn't a viable way to share your file to your clients or colleagues. Your clients and colleagues would need to have an Office 365 Excel 2019 build in order to open the file. This is also counter intuitive to sharing the file over a uniform platform.

Ultimately, in editing mode, you will have to deal with several versions of the same file. To keep down file management, it is better to only share Read-Only files. If you must use a file management scheme, we suggest labeling your files with the date that they were edited. For example, if today's date was 10-14-18 and you just saved an instance of our example file with your work, then the name of the file would be $EastNorthCentralFTWorkers\_[10 - 14 - 18].xlsx$.

Chapter 3

Automation and Efficiency

1. Data" sheet

2. Go to the "Usual Weekly Earnings" column, cell $F5$

3. After computing $F5$, copy-paste to the rest of the column to randomize the data.

4. Go to the **Summary Stats** sheet and click on one of the pivot tables

5. Update the tables to reflect this change by going to:

$$PivotTable\ Analyze > Data > Refresh\ drop-down >$$
$$Refresh\ All$$

6. Save your progress and note the location of the modified file.

Power Pivot Navigational Shortcuts

Navigation shortcuts reduce the time spent on searching for different buttons and tasks. You must learn these shortcuts to incorporate these shortcuts into your computations. Typically, if they save you time, you will naturally use them, like the traditional $[CTRL] + [C], [CTRL] + [V]$ for copy-paste in Windows.

Here is a table of keyboard shortcuts and their function in Power Pivot ("Power Pivot keyboard shortcuts and accessibility—Office Support," n.d.).

Note:

Power Pivot is only available in Windows desktop builds. Therefore, this table is only for Windows keyboard shortcuts.

Table: Power Pivot Navigation Keyboard Shortcuts
This table lists keyboard shortcuts and how they behave in the Power Pivot widget. This table has been categorized for your convenience. The "Basic Computation & Navigation" category, for example, includes many shortcuts which you may already recognize, but explicitly lists how they behave in Power Pivot. The other categories include table navigation shortcuts followed by lesser known computation shortcuts.

Category: Basic Navigation & Computation

Key Combination	Description
$[Mouse: Right - Click]$	After selecting an item, **open the context menu** for the selected item (cell, column, or row).
$[CTRL] + [A]$	Select the entire table (**all** for entire).
$[CTRL] + [C]$	**Copy** selected data
$[CTRL] + [D]$	**Delete** the table.
$[CTRL] + [M]$	**Move** the table.
$[CTRL] + [R]$	**Rename** the table.
$[CTRL] + [S]$	**Save** the table.
$[CTRL] + [Y]$	**Redo** the last action.
$[CTRL] + [Z]$	**Undo** the last action.
$[CTRL] + [Space - bar]$	Select the current **column**.

[SHIFT] + [Space − bar]	Select the current **row**.

Category: Table Navigation	
Key Combination	Description
[SHIFT] + [Pg Up]	Selects all cells from the current location to the **first cell** of the column.
[SHIFT] + [Pg Dn]	Selects all cells from the current location to the **last cell** of the column.
[SHIFT] + [END]	Select all cells from the current location to the **last cell** of the row.
[SHIFT] + [HOME]	Select all cells from the current location to the **first cell** of the row.
[CTRL] + [Pg Up]	**Move** to the previous table
[CTRL] + [Pg Dn]	**Move** to the next table
[CTRL] + [HOME]	Move to the first cell in the **upper left corner** of the selected table
[CTRL] + [END]	Move to the last cell in the **lower right corner** of the selected table (or the last row of the 'Add Column')
[CTRL] + [Left − Arrow]	**Move** to the first cell of the selected row.
[CTRL] + [Right − Arrow]	**Move** to the last cell of the selected row.
[CTRL] + [Up − Arrow]	**Move** to the first cell of the selected column.

$[CTRL] + [Down - Arrow]$	**Move** to the last cell of the selected column.

Category: Other Computation Shortcuts	
Key Combination	Description
$[CTRL] + [ESC]$	**Close or cancel.** Can be for closing a dialog box or canceling a process such as a paste operation.
$[F5]$	Open **Go To** Dialog Box
$[F9]$	**Recalculate** all formulas in the Power Pivot window.

Automate PivotTables with Macros in VBA

Power users of Excel know how to use macros to handle repetitive tasks. Macros are small, custom programs that you can execute in Excel. The programs are written in VBA (Visual Basic for Applications).

Note:

In many online resources macros and VBA are used interchangeably. Macros are the executable script of instructions. VBA is the platform used to write a macro.

In order to use a macro, you must:

1. Enable the developer ribbon in Excel

2. Save the workbook as a "macro enabled file"

The workbook file must be macro-enabled to implement them. Microsoft established this "macro-enabled" file type for all of their products, including Excel, in order to prevent malicious macros from hijacking computer systems though VBA. This is why many offices outright ban macro enabled files. At the bare minimum, Microsoft will always prompt you when you are about to open any macro enabled file.

The best policy for creating automated Excel sheets is to have a single, "production PC", a desktop that is able to run macros. The resulting data and tables should be saved to a regular Excel workbook. When creating macros, keep this format in mind.

The VBA console, called Visual Basic Editor (VBE) by the Microsoft Support website, can be accessed using $[ALT] + [F11]$ in PC . To access the VBE console in Mac, the keyboard shortcut is $[Option] + [F11]$]. However, the "Developer Ribbon" must be enabled to run and set up shortcuts for running your macros.

Accessing the Developer Ribbon in Windows and Mac

The ribbon must be enabled on the main tabs menu. In order to achieve this in Windows do the following steps:

1. Go to *File > Options > Customize Ribbon*

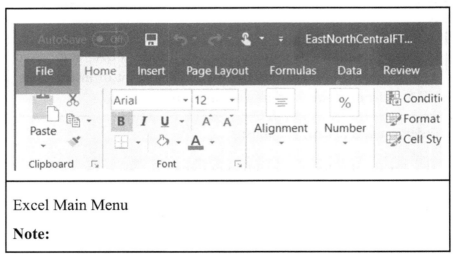

Excel Main Menu

Note:

> Most actions start here. Remember that you can only access this menu when you have an active file opened.

2. Check the "Developer's" box on the right and click **OK**

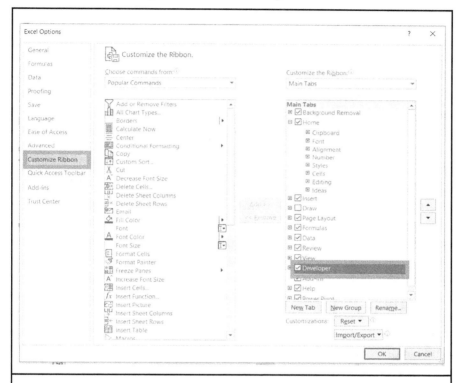

Target for Excel Options: Customize Ribbon >Main Tabs

This screenshot depicts the target window for the Customize Ribbons section. By default, Developer is disabled. However, it is considered part of the Main Tabs in Microsoft.

The Developer ribbon should appear. This ribbon gives you a variety of tools for managing your Excel sheet, including Active X controls. However, your file must be macro-enabled to use these tools due to the security concerns discussed prior.

Developer Ribbon

This screenshot depicts the resulting Developer ribbon. There are several advanced tools used to automate your Microsoft outfit across several of their platforms. We will be focusing only on building and managing macros.

The steps are similar in Mac OS Excel 2019 builds. You can access the VBA compiler on a Mac through:

$Opt + F11$ or $Fn + Opt + F11$

The macro manager can be accessed on Mac using:

$OPTION + F8$

Starting with Macros: Learning VBA Syntax

This text focuses on pivottables; therefore, we will be discussing common pivottable oriented macros. To begin using VBA you must first learn this language syntax. Consider the following Pivot Table code pulled from a macro demonstration resource ("The VBA Guide To Excel Pivot Tables," n.d.).

```
 1    Sub CreatePivotTable()
 2    'PURPOSE: Creates a brand new Pivot table on a new worksheet from data in the ActiveSheet
 3    'Source: www.TheSpreadsheetGuru.com
 4
 5    Dim sht As Worksheet
 6    Dim pvtCache As PivotCache
 7    Dim pvt As PivotTable
 8    Dim StartPvt As String
 9    Dim SrcData As String
10
11    'Determine the data range you want to pivot
12        SrcData = ActiveSheet.Name & "!" & Range("A1:R100").Address(ReferenceStyle:=xlR1C1)
13
14    'Create a new worksheet
15        Set sht = Sheets.Add
16
17    'Where do you want Pivot Table to start?
18        StartPvt = sht.Name & "!" & sht.Range("A3").Address(ReferenceStyle:=xlR1C1)
19
20    'Create Pivot Cache from Source Data
21        Set pvtCache = ActiveWorkbook.PivotCaches.Create( _
22            SourceType:=xlDatabase, _
23            SourceData:=SrcData)
24
25    'Create Pivot table from Pivot Cache
26        Set pvt = pvtCache.CreatePivotTable( _
27            TableDestination:=StartPvt, _
28            TableName:="PivotTable1")
29
30    End Sub
```

Code Snippet: Create a Pivot Table

Screenshot of the code in VBA. In many cases you will be modifying code pulled from Excel help sites. To use these effectively, you should learn how to read them.

1. Sub CreatePivotTable()

This is the calling function for the macro. This is important when deploying macro in other macro. All functions take the form of "name"(arguments), if the function takes any arguments. This should be familiar because this is how we call formula functions in Excel.

2. 'PURPOSE: Creates a brand new Pivot table on a new worksheet from data...

3. 'Source: www.TheSpreadsheetGuru.com

These are comments. Comments are indicated with a backtick `and are not compiled with the rest of the code. They are used to include notes in

273

the code to make reading the code comprehensible. The programmer of the macro was thorough enough to explain each action using comments.

Dim sht As Worksheet

Dim pvtCache As PivotCache

. ..

Dim SrcData As String

This is where the variables of the program are declared. These variables are used to carry out the operations of the program. This section is useful in identifying what parts of the program to edit because it also tells you the type of variable. Thus, if you wanted to change some aspect of the program, you would begin here.

After the declaration of variables is the main body of the program, this is where all of the instructions are listed. This programmer explained each section of code and what it does. Some instructions you would want to change are **line 12** and **line 18**, as they determine the range used to create a pivot table and where the resulting pivot table will populate. In this case, this macro operates only on the active worksheet in the window.

Common VBA Automated Pivot Table Actions: Create a Pivot Table

Let's modify our example code for our purposes. Deploying this macro will create a new pivottable in one click from a named range.

1. Save a copy of the workbook as macro enabled workbook with the name:

EastNorthCentralFTWorkers_Macro.xlsm

Note:

Actions executed by macros are not saved in the undo-redo cache. This means that any action a macro executes cannot be undone. Further, macro-enabled files cannot be autosaved. This makes it difficult to obtain recent past versions of the file. *If you are testing and developing macros, it is best practice to always save a separate macro-enabled file.*

2. Use the shortcut to access the Macro dialogue box

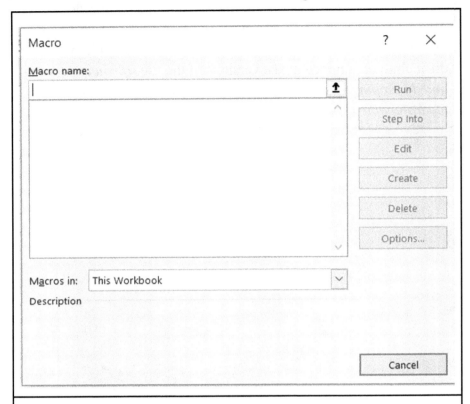

Macro Dialogue Box

Screenshot of the Macro dialogue box. This dialogue box is used to manage, run, and create macro. Once this box is populated with macro you can assign custom shortcut keys to each macro by going to the **Options** button.

3. Type in *CreatePivotTable* into the macro box and click **Create**. This will start an instance of VBA in a new window

4. Copy the following into VBA:

```
Sub CreatePivotTable()
Dim sht As Worksheet
Dim pvtCache As PivotCache
Dim pvt As PivotTable
Dim StartPvt As String
Dim SrcData As String


'Determine the data range you want to pivot
'This part of the code was changed for our pivottable
  SrcData = ActiveSheet.Name & "!" &
Range("A4:H6370").Address(ReferenceStyle:=Pivot_Table_Values)



'Create a new worksheet
  Set sht = Sheets.Add



'Where do you want Pivot Table to start?
  StartPvt = sht.Name & "!" &
sht.Range("A3").Address(ReferenceStyle:=xlR1C1)
```

```
'Create Pivot Cache from Source Data

 Set pvtCache = ActiveWorkbook.PivotCaches.Create( _

  SourceType:=xlDatabase, _

  SourceData:=SrcData)


'Create Pivot table from Pivot Cache

 Set pvt = pvtCache.CreatePivotTable( _

  TableDestination:=StartPvt, _

  TableName:="PivotTableTest")

End Sub
```

5. Click save and to execute your macro, click the small green triangle to run

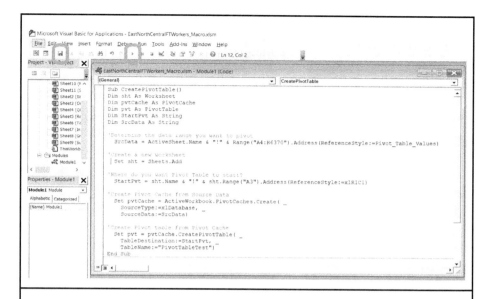

Microsoft VBA Editor

This is a screenshot of the VBA editor. This allows you to create, edit, and execute macro. In this code, you must be on the **Data** sheet in order to execute. Otherwise, the macro will give you an error. As this is programming, all instructions must be very verbose. Any errors in syntax or addressing will generate a "Debugging" prompt. To see this prompt, try changing one of the variables in the declaration portion of the code and running the macro.

6. After the Macro executes, it will create a new sheet and a new pivot table that you can populate manually.

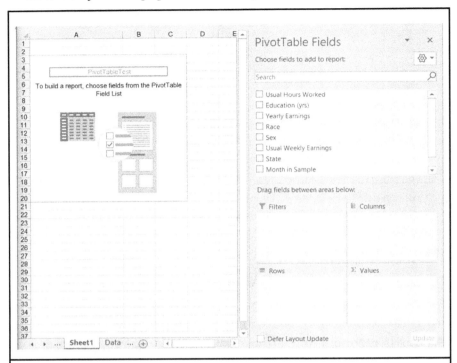

Target: Macro Generated PivotTable

This is a screenshot of the new sheet generated by *Sub CreatePivotTable()*. This macro allows us to automatically create pivottable with a keyboard shortcut instead of manually selecting items each time. This is particularly useful for repetitive reports that use the same, named ranges every time.

Following are some similar pivottable automation codes that automate with pivottable management. Create these macros on this file and explore them yourself ("The VBA Guide To Excel Pivot Tables," n.d.):

Delete a Specific Pivot Table

```vba
Sub DeletePivotTable()
'PURPOSE: How to delete a specific Pivot Table
'SOURCE: www.TheSpreadsheetGuru.com


'Delete Pivot Table By Name
  ActiveSheet.PivotTables("PivotTable1").TableRange2.Clear


End Sub
```

Note:

The *DeletePivotTable*() macro requires that you have your pivottables named. You can name your pivot tables by selecting them and going to:

*PivotTable Analyze > PivotTable drop − down
> "PivotTable Name"*

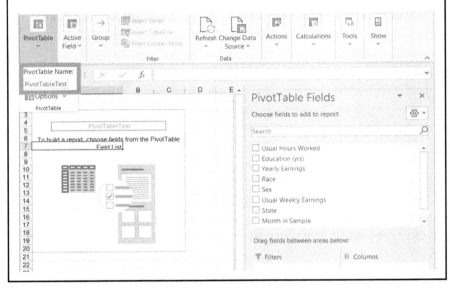

```
Delete All Pivot Tables

Sub DeleteAllPivotTables()
'PURPOSE: Delete all Pivot Tables in your Workbook
'SOURCE: www.TheSpreadsheetGuru.com


Dim sht As Worksheet
Dim pvt As PivotTable


'Loop Through Each Pivot Table In Currently Viewed Workbook
  For Each sht In ActiveWorkbook.Worksheets
    For Each pvt In sht.PivotTables
      pvt.TableRange2.Clear
    Next pvt
  Next sht


End Sub
```

This code is useful for cleaning up workbooks after your analysis. However, it is ill advised to assign *Sub DeleteAllPivotTables*() and similar macros like it to keyboard shortcut. Actions by macro cannot be undone and this macro can potentially destroy your work.

Common VBA Automated Pivot Table Actions: Modifying Fields

Before creating macros that automate fields you must have an understanding of what fields are. Pivottable fields are populated when you create a pivottable from a range. Excel recognizes fields to manipulate them, usually the top row of a column that describes the data below as in our example. Recall from the multiple ranges consolidation that the old pivot table wizard only recognizes up to 4 fields.

Conversely, you can program macros to manage fields if the data is going to have the same structure. Recall from earlier in the chapter our conversation about modularization. Having a modular macro means that each task is handled by only one macro. Calling these macro in a full script, a list macro executed together, you can potentially create a pivottable with a few keyboard shortcuts in a few seconds.

Logically in your script, after executing*CreatePivotTable*(), you can manage the fields with macros and generate a report in seconds.

Let's look at *Adding_PivotFields*().

Similar to the *CreatePivotTable*()macro, this macro must be edited for the context of your dataset. Let's look at a numbered version of the code to analyze it.

```
1    Sub Adding_PivotFields()
2    'PURPOSE: Show how to add various Pivot Fields to Pivot Table
3    'SOURCE: www.TheSpreadsheetGuru.com
4
5    Dim pvt As PivotTable
6
7    Set pvt = ActiveSheet.PivotTables("PivotTable1")
8
9        'Add item to the Report Filter
10       pvt.PivotFields("Year").Orientation = xlPageField
11
12       'Add item to the Column Labels
13       pvt.PivotFields("Month").Orientation = xlColumnField
14
15       'Add item to the Row Labels
16       pvt.PivotFields("Account").Orientation = xlRowField
17
18       'Position Item in list
19       pvt.PivotFields("Year").Position = 1
20
21       'Format Pivot Field
22       pvt.PivotFields("Year").NumberFormat = "#,##0"
23
24       'Turn on Automatic updates/calculations --like screenupdating to speed up code
25       pvt.ManualUpdate = False
26
27   End Sub
```

Annotated VBA Language: Adding_PivotFields()

This is a screenshot of *Adding_PivotFields*(). You may have noticed that this screenshot does not look the same as the VBA

284

editor. This shot was taken using Notepad ++, a free text program for editing code. Notepad++ annotates the text in any language of your choice and also provides line numbers, where the current VBA does not. As VBA is not always available due to security concerns, Notepad++ is an excellent text editor for editing and studying code when you do not have access to VBA. However, you need VBA to compile and debug the code.

Adding_PivotFields()sorts predefined fields into a predefined pivot table named*pivotable*1. Let's return to our first simple pivot table example. It called for "Sex" in the rows and the average of "Usual Hours Worked". We are targeting our new pivottable in the newly created sheet, so we will have to change the predefined pivottable name to *PivotTableTest* . Thus, our new code for *Adding_PivotFields*()would be:

[Modified] Add Pivot Fields

```
Sub Adding_PivotFields()
'PURPOSE: Show how to add various Pivot Fields to Pivot Table
'SOURCE: www.TheSpreadsheetGuru.com


Dim pvt As PivotTable


Set pvt = ActiveSheet.PivotTables("PivotTableTest")


'Add item to the Report Filter
   'pvt.PivotFields("Year").Orientation = xlPageField--
Unnecessary


 'Add item to the Column Labels
   'pvt.PivotFields("Month").Orientation = xlColumnField--
Unnecessary


 'Add item to the Row Labels
   pvt.PivotFields("Sex").Orientation = xlRowField
```

```
'Position Item in list

  'pvt.PivotFields("Year").Position = 1 --Unnecessary



 'Add Values Item in list

  pvt.AddDataField pvt.PivotFields("Usual Hours Worked"),
"Average of Usual Hours Worked", xlAverage



 'Format Pivot Field

 ' pvt.PivotFields("Year").NumberFormat = "#,##0" --
Unnecessary



 'Turn on Automatic updates/calculations --like screenupdating to
speed up code

  pvt.ManualUpdate = False


End Sub
```

Note:

In this modified code we kept the old lines and commented them out. This is good for keeping track of changes in your macros. However, this can lead to a lot of junk code in your macros. Once you are done developing your macros, clean up your comments. Make sure the comments are clear and describe each part of the code.

To execute this code, return to the newly generated sheet with the pivottable entitled *PivotTableTest*. Go to: *Developer > Macros > Macro Name*: *Adding_PivotFields* and click the **Run** button. This will populate the empty *PivotTableTest*table.

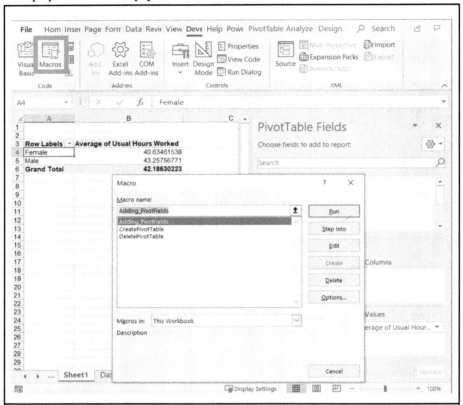

Editing the "PivotTestTable" PivotTable with Macros

This is a screenshot of the resulting pivottable after populating it with *Adding_PivotFields*(). After establishing the code, it only took seconds for Excel to generate this data with a new pivottable. The best way to deploy these macros in a modular way is to create a script that deploys *CreatePivotTable*() first and *Adding_PivotFields*() second.

This code combines some of the other operators and arguments at the SpreadsheetGuru's list of common macro codes. Following are some similar pivottable field management macros. Study them on your own and use them to modify your pivottables:

Add Calculated Pivot Fields

```
Sub AddCalculatedField()
'PURPOSE: Add a calculated field to a pivot table
'SOURCE: www.TheSpreadsheetGuru.com


Dim pvt As PivotTable
Dim pf As PivotField


'Set Variable to Desired Pivot Table
  Set pvt = ActiveSheet.PivotTables("PivotTable1")


'Set Variable Equal to Desired Calculated Pivot Field
  For Each pf In pvt.PivotFields
    If pf.SourceName = "Inflation" Then Exit For
  Next


'Add Calculated Field to Pivot Table
  pvt.AddDataField pf


End Sub
```

```
Add A Values Field

Sub AddValuesField()
'PURPOSE: Add A Values Field to a Pivot Table
'SOURCE: www.TheSpreadsheetGuru.com


Dim pvt As PivotTable
Dim pf As String
Dim pf_Name As String


pf = "Salaries"
pf_Name = "Sum of Salaries"


Set pvt = ActiveSheet.PivotTables("PivotTable1")


pvt.AddDataField pvt.PivotFields("Salaries"), pf_Name, xlSum


End Sub
```

This example *AddValuesField*()macro code deploys xl consolidation functions to instruct the *Σ Values* section on what calculation to perform. In the plainest of terms, these are VBA arguments that allow you to automate different calculations in the Value field. They are fairly comprensible and the most common ones you will use are ("XlConsolidationFunction enumeration (Excel) | Microsoft Docs," n.d.):

xlAverage: Finds the average

xlCount: Finds the number of entries

xlCountNums: Find the number of entries that are numerical

xlSum: Sum, which is the default calculation when setting a Values with VBA

You can find a whole list of other arguments at the Microsoft VBA support site.

Chapter 4

Analysis

Analysis is the process of evaluating data and creating new perspective of that data. Those who get the most out of data analysis are those who understand the investigative process. Unfortunately, many people tend to mistake Excel and pivot tables to be the primary tool for creating these new perspectives. These tools may allow you to create a presentation. The impact of that presentation, however, depends on your grasp of the analysis and the way you present your content. This distinction separates data entry freelancers from business analyst consultants who inform business decisions.

One natural approach to analysis is asking the right questions. In this chapter, we will discuss the process of analysis and overview some features that will assist in presenting your analysis. Recall our discussion of functionality. Pivottables, and Power Pivot wizards, are features that allow you to achieve a specific goal: creating new perspectives of large swaths of what would otherwise be unintelligible spreadsheet tables of information.

After completing this chapter, you will be able to:

- Gather and arranging data for evaluation

- Reason context for investigation and evaluation

- Create new perspectives on the data

Finally, we will briefly overview data mining: using tech to pull trends from large data sets.

292

Overview: Process of Analysis

Pivottables allow you to view data in different ways, which enables you to analyze and report on large amounts of data in a meaningful way. Analysis, therefore, is broken down into 3 steps:

1. **Providing Context**: Gathering and arranging data in a meaningful way

2. **Evaluating**: Asking questions about the data

3. **Creating**: Discovering and validating new perspectives on the data

Excel allows an analysis of large data sets through aggregating them with pivot tables and slicers. Pivot tables are a tool that allows you to gather and assemble data from large data sets. Recall the section on accessing multiple consolidation ranges. By using the keyboard shortcuts ()in Windows, (in Mac: [⌘] + [⌥] + [P]), you can open the Pivot Table Wizard. This allows you direct access to the consolidation ranges feature.

Meanwhile, slicers allow you to instantly change and filter multiple pivot tables. Slicers are also available through the Pivot Table wizard once you have multiple pivot tables. While this feature allows you to control multiple pivot tables, the slicer's *functionality* are the different perspectives it creates to achieve better visibility into data.

> **Note:**
>
> Slicers are only available on the desktop version. Therefore, they can only be viewed in Excel for the web.

Providing Context: Creating and Managing Multiple Pivot Tables

Slicers allow you to filter table and pivot table data. Most importantly, slicers clearly label filtered states, making the tables more presentable in reports. To use slicers for pivottables the following conditions must be met ("Use slicers to filter data—Office Support," n.d.):

1. You need to be on a desktop build of Excel

2. PivotTables need to be enabled

3. The data must be in a PivotTable

4. Must not be in compatible mode

Note:

In order to save our example file, Excel put the file into compatibility mode. This is done for files that may be viewed on different machines. To get your file out of compatibility mode you must go to *File > Info > Compatibility Mode*

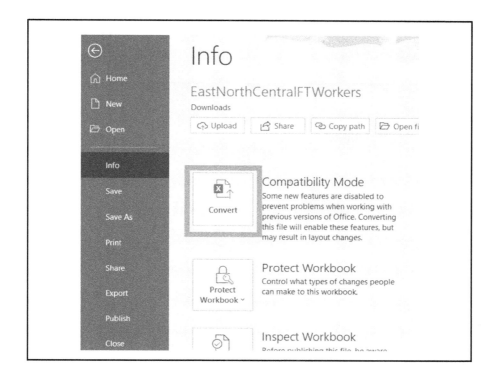

After all these conditions are met, the best way to see the value of slicers is to have multiple PivotTables. Let's return to our large dataset example. The Q&A asks for 3 different pivot tables. Let's rearrange our Summary Stats page into a report by state.

1. Rearrange the tables using *PivotTable Analyze > Action > Move Table*...for each item

Note:
This is also a good time to name each table. The suggested names are:

Avg_Y_Earnings

Avg_Hours_Worked

Avg_Hours_Worked

Keep track of these names. This is how the slicer will control the pivottables

2. Select a pivot table

3. Go to *Insert* > *"Filters"* > *Slicer*

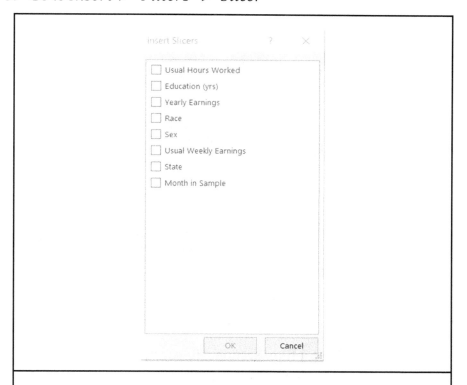

Insert Slicers ? ✕

☐ Usual Hours Worked
☐ Education (yrs)
☐ Yearly Earnings
☐ Race
☐ Sex
☐ Usual Weekly Earnings
☐ State
☐ Month in Sample

OK   Cancel

Slicer Dialogue Box

This is a screenshot of the slicer dialogue box. The slicers automatically connect to the dataset through the pivottable. Since these are essentially filters, it is better to choose fields that are independent variables: location, race, sex, and education. In this case, we are choosing location, "State".

4. Click on **State**

5. Select the slicer to make the Slicer Ribbon appear and navigate to *Slicer* > *Report Connections*

6. Select all PivotTables

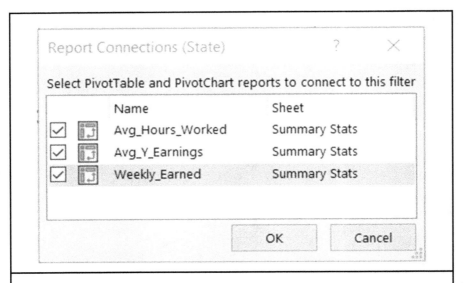

Report Connections Dialogue Box

This is a screenshot of the controls for the State slicer.

Note:

All pivot tables have a filter section. However, this filter section is limited to the individual pivottable. Using slicers allow you to deploy multiple pivot tables in interactive reports.

7. Save your progress

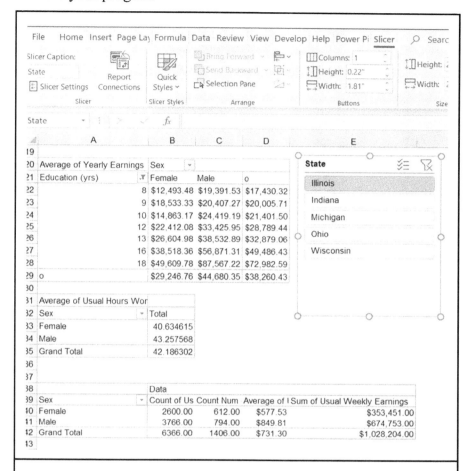

Target: State Slicer

This is a screenshot of the resulting slicer after selecting state. The Slicer ribbon also appears, where you can manage what pivottables your slicer controls.

Creating: Discovering and Validating New Perspectives on the Data

Similar to filters with regular Excel spreadsheets, slicers allow you to slice data into various views instantly. Manipulating the data helps with finding new perspectives.

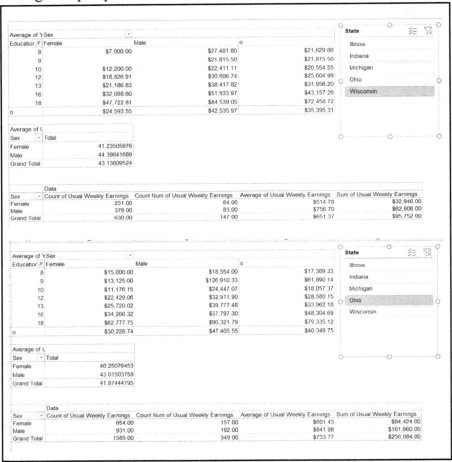

Average of Y Sex

Education	Female	Male	o
8	$7,000.00	$27,481.80	$21,629.86
9		$21,815.50	$21,815.50
10	$12,200.00	$22,411.11	$20,554.55
12	$18,826.91	$30,606.74	$25,604.99
13	$21,186.83	$38,417.82	$31,956.20
16	$32,098.60	$51,933.97	$43,157.26
18	$47,722.81	$84,539.05	$72,458.72
o	$24,593.55	$42,535.97	$35,395.31

State: Illinois, Indiana, Michigan, Ohio, **Wisconsin**

Average of U

Sex	Total
Female	41.23505976
Male	44.39841689
Grand Total	43.13809524

Sex	Count of Usual Weekly Earnings	Count Num of Usual Weekly Earnings	Average of Usual Weekly Earnings	Sum of Usual Weekly Earnings
Female	251.00	64.00	$514.78	$32,946.00
Male	379.00	83.00	$756.70	$62,806.00
Grand Total	630.00	147.00	$651.37	$95,752.00

Average of Y Sex

Education	Female	Male	o
8	$15,000.00	$18,554.00	$17,389.33
9	$13,125.00	$126,910.33	$61,890.14
10	$11,176.15	$24,447.07	$18,057.37
12	$22,429.06	$32,911.90	$28,580.15
13	$25,720.02	$39,777.48	$33,962.18
16	$34,266.32	$57,797.30	$48,304.69
18	$62,777.75	$90,321.79	$79,335.12
o	$30,228.74	$47,405.55	$40,349.75

State: Illinois, Indiana, Michigan, **Ohio**, Wisconsin

Average of U

Sex	Total
Female	40.25076453
Male	43.01503759
Grand Total	41.87444795

Sex	Count of Usual Weekly Earnings	Count Num of Usual Weekly Earnings	Average of Usual Weekly Earnings	Sum of Usual Weekly Earnings
Female	654.00	157.00	$601.43	$94,424.00
Male	931.00	192.00	$841.98	$161,660.00
Grand Total	1585.00	349.00	$733.77	$256,084.00

Comparison of Wisconsin and Ohio Reports

Looking at the State data side by side, you can see that there is a gap for Females with 9 years of education in Wisconsin. Recall our misleading scatter plot example. How might you represent this gap in the data? Further, consider the quality of the data. Is this gap due to less rigorous sample size? What portion of the report would support this assertion?

Analysis can be used to model results in a way that is both visually attractive and effective. Recall our conversation about analysis and creating new perspectives. These perspectives are more easily discovered when visualized.

Chapter 5

Investigative Modeling using Pivot Charts

I f you were paying attention, you would notice that we only discussed two aspects of analysis in chapter 4, providing context and creation. However, in the overview of analysis, we stated that there were 3 steps in the process:

1. **Providing Context**: Gathering and arranging data in a meaningful way

2. **Evaluating**: Asking questions about the data

3. **Creating**: Discovering and validating new perspectives on the data

Evaluation of data depends solely on the type of data you are analyzing and, therefore, deserves its own chapter. Aspects of evaluation and investigation for all sorts of datasets are found in data modeling. Modeling data is an important step for creating new perspectives on data. It allows you to visibly see the data in a meaningful way and investigate through a series of informed questions. The majority of these questions are "how" and "why" questions, since the others (what, when, who) can already be answered by the charts of data in front of you.

After you've investigated and found your conclusions, modeling is also critical for communicating these perspectives on data. For the audiences that you are presenting your information to, modeling is often the only way to communicate your findings. More information can be gleaned from a visualization like a chart or a graph than from numbers from a table.

The communicative property of visualization is particularly the case for large data sets. For big data, which can be several thousand rows and columns, data can only be presented with a map. This chapter will cover basic principles in data modeling, creating visualizations, and building maps.

Principals in Data Modeling

When using modeling to investigate data, a chart or a graph is more adept at answering "how" and "why" questions. For example, consider our large data set. This dataset can technically answer all the other non-analysis questions on its own with the help of a few filters and a formula. For example:

"Who"
Do men who have greater than 12 years of education make more than [Y] dollars?

"Where"
Where are women least likely to make less than [Y] dollars?

"When"
Given the month in sample, when do the highest ranges occur?

"What"
What is the lowest earning in each state?

However, if we were to generate a few linear regressions over an (X,Y) plane, then we could answer questions such as:

"How do years of education [X] determine yearly salary [Y] for females"?

If in our theoretical graph the line goes [up], it would indicate that [Y] had an increase over the years of [X]. This is the value that modeling brings to analysis: it provides trends that tell us "how" things happen and may even glean "why" things happen with a little more context.

Ergo, charts tracking several items are more prepared to answer "why" since we can compare the axises to each other and comment on causality. However, you must be careful with this line of questioning in statistics. More context is usually needed to confirm acertations of "why," usually confirming with contextual research such as interviews. Acertainations gleaned from statistical analysis are still useful because they can inform a beginning hypothesis for you to test. Even more importantly, there are rules in modeling to ensure that presented data can give you the most accurate acertaintions to test.

Charts that are incorrectly modeled can skew data and, therefore, can skew insights. This can be disastrous for analysts, since they can easily come to the wrong conclusions. When we move on to presenting our data, being a data analyst requires a level of integrity: charts can visually skew data for audiences as well. Analysts who use this knowledge to purposefully skew charts to confirm their worldview lack scientific integrity. Knowing these modeling rules can help you recognize human error as well as purposeful meddling. Following these rules ensures accurate modeling:

1. **Use an expected range on the independent axis.** The independent axis is the "X" axis on charts. This axis usually represents units of time or some other independent variable. Always start the graph at 0 or at "time-zero" as the marked beginning of your dataset. The x-axis should always be increasing. Do not "break" the independent axis, i.e. you must have a continuous number line starting from zero. If you have a large gap in the [Y] axis from your starting point, instead, use a rate that accurately reflects the data. Excel's charts and graphs do this automatically for you.

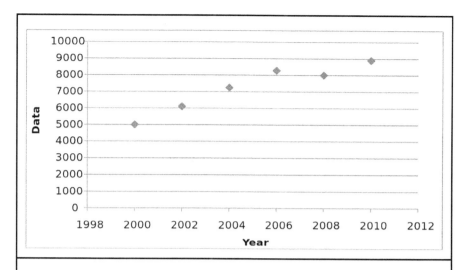

Scatterplot with a broken Independent axis: Missing Values

This is an example of a graph with a broken X axis. More specifically, this dataset is a scatter plot with all of the odd years removed ("File:Scatter Plot with missing categories.svg—Wikimedia Commons," n.d.). As a scatter plot, all data points on the graph must be represented by a point. If the value for 1999 was zero, for example, it must be included. Removing the odd "Years," not only breaks the X axis, it removes 50% of the data, which makes this graph broken.

2. **Use an expected range on the dependent axis.** Dependent axis is usually the item you're measuring or topic of the graph. Don't 'break' the dependent axis. Use a rate that accurately reflects the data.

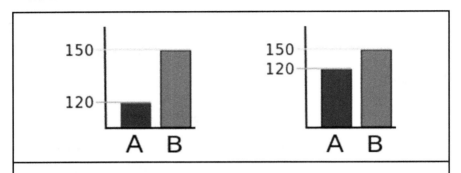

Bar Graph with no defined range

This is a side by side comparison of a graph representing undefined Y axis. Technically both A and B are the same same values. However, there is no point representing zero and there is no established rate of increase ("Bar graph missing zero1—Misleading graph—Wikipedia," n.d.; "File:Example truncated bar graph.svg—Wikimedia Commons," n.d.).

3. **Clearly label units**: percentages, currency, time, etc

4. Percentages should always add up to 100% on a pie chart

   a. Exception: Rate of increase, e.g. some item increased [Y%] over [X] time

   b. Rate of increase will always be over time, and therefore, will be represented on a graph, not a pie chart.

   c. Be sure to label clearly the period of time for each increase

   d. The rate of time will be uniform, i.e., 1 year

5. **Always use a descriptive title**: .e.g. "Measurement of [Y] over [X] for [Length of X]"

Visualization rules always depend on what sort of data you're representing. Recall the listed rule about percentages. Percentages are a ratio, a method of showing relation between data points without getting hung up on the value of numbers. A value of 100 is greater than 7, for example, but with percentages we know that 100 is 93% greater than 7. This example is easy because 100 is a 'clean' number that is easier to comprehend, like all the powers of 10. However, when you change the values to numbers you are more likely to see in the wild, $171.64 increasing to $2,452.00, the 93% increase is easier to graph.

Taking this example, how to represent this data is dependent on the context. This 93% increase is easier shown on a graph if it occured over time. Conversely, if the data is accompanied by other values that are part of a whole, it would be more appropriate to represent them with a pie chart, which visually demonstrates the values' relation to one another. If the $171.64 instead represented expenditures of a $2,452.00 budget, an easier way to express this relation is with a 7% slice of a pie.

That being said, the rules above mainly focus on general best practices for X,Y graphs: bar charts, line charts, and other graphs with axes. Some of these items apply to other charts, like 3 through 5. To ensure the integrity of your models, you should review the rules for other charts that are available on Excel such as sunburst or whisker plots. Due to the impact of inaccurate investigative modeling, Excel has guides for charts and graphs using wizards. The next sections will cover how to use these wizards for accurate modeling.

Creating Visualizations

In the Q&A, the course asks students to create a bar graph and a demographics table. However, these require variables outside of our focus. For now, we will create a two visualizations comparing the state of Wisconsin and the state of Ohio.

1. Select the *Avg_Y_Earnings* pivottable

2. Go to *Insert > PivotChart > Column* and select **Clustered Column**

The fields are already propagated for you in the wizard

3. Select **OK**

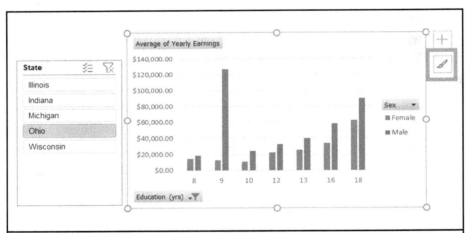

Target: Ohio Bar Graph

This screenshot depicts the Pivot Chart generated after the listed steps. It can be toggled between any of the five listed states with the slicer depicted alongside. Selecting the paintbrush allows you to modify the appearance of the chart. The plus sign lets you toggle the various chart elements on and off such as different axises, their titles, and even including a trend line. The graph can also be isolated along either independent variable (Sex, Education).

4. Save your progress

Interpreting Data using Visualizations

A large part of modeling is reporting on data. In the last chapter we covered modeling as an investigative tool in analysis. Rendering these models accurately can give you visual insight into how and why data behaves. This creates a model so you can analyze the data properly.

However, simply copying and pasting your models for presentation is not enough. To report your findings to others requires additional steps, including arranging models and data in a meaningful way to convey your findings. Many of these steps are dependent on your client, but the majority of these steps involve providing context for your visualizations. This context and composition is important for pointing people to the correct conclusions. Take, for example, our previous example studying the different perspectives of the data broken down by state. By including the State slicer and connecting it to all of the created pivottables, we have created a dynamic dashboard that can be toggled between all 5 states.

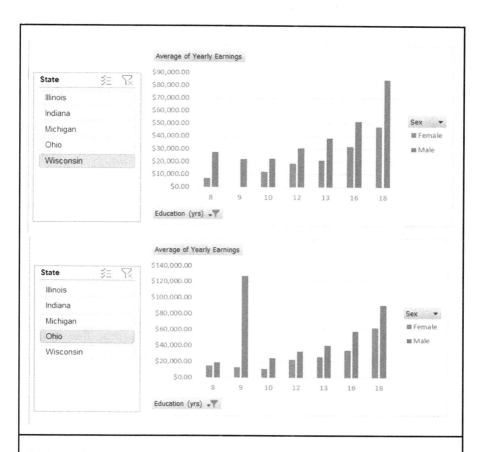

Ohio and Wisconsin Pivot Chart Comparison

These two screenshots are two shots of a dynamic pivot chart broken down by state. Recall our side by side comparison of the Pivottables in an earlier section. Also recall the question about representing the gap in the Wisconsin data. Are they well represented using this bar graph?

In the previous section about analysis we discussed at length the need for "how" and "why" questions to complete analysis. With these detailed charts and graphs, we can easily postulate about why the aspect of the data occurs. For example, one possible question inspired by the Wisconsin pivottable was "Why is there a gap in the data for females with only 9 years of education?" Looking at the total count of data for Wisconsin, one can hypothesize that it is due to the small sample size in comparison with another state like Ohio. Just looking at the total values, Ohio had roughly three times as many females reporting than Wisconsin. Comparing 200 indivuals to 600, that is a difference of about 400 indivuals.

However, looking at the pivottables, it is difficult to make a conclusion about trends. It is only when the data is properly visualized that we can come to some conclusions. Datasets with a small population size tend to have chaotic trends. This is because there are fewer individual data points that could lend themselves to a smooth trend. Therefore, it is difficult to identify a curve or a pattern with smaller population sizes. Going by this reasoning, we would expect that Wisconsin would have no identifiable shapes or trends.

With this hypothesis and comparing it to the actual data, the opposite seems to be true. Wisconsin, despite the lack of females in one of its data points, has a more identifiable shape. The bars form a rolling hill shape indicating a healthy dataset. There may be no data at this datapoint because of how narrowly the chart is broken down. There simply may have been no females with only 9 years of education who reported a salary.

Ohio, in contrast, has one large outlier, particularly at 9 years of education. There could be several reasons for this, including industry trends within Ohio. For example, there could be a large push for high paying positions that don't require a college degree, such as union jobs where people progress to higher pay grades on seniority. Someone who started working earlier and did not attend college would, therefore, make more money in this scenario. The only way to confirm this is through investigative research such as interviews, or looking at additional variables such as age.

One possible approach to research is to get more data. This dataset was originally collected in March 1999. There have been several censuses conducted since then. Further, getting and cleaning the data would be easy with the skills we have practiced. After converting the worksheet to a template, we can generate recorded variables using the formulas already in the sheet. Further, you can build macros to generate pivot tables since the data will be structured in the same way. Finally, you could build dynamic self-service reporting systems through macro, even comparing the different census datasets with one another.

Chapter 6

Troubleshooting

This final chapter will cover troubleshooting scenarios. Thesce solutions are indexed by the scenarios that they address. This chapter will also refer to the associated activity or demonstration, which is good for practicing work arounds.

Power Pivot Ribbon Disappears

Sometimes your Add-ins may disappear if Excel restarts itself. To restore the Power Pivot Ribbon in your main menu, follow this step by step solution from Microsoft ("Start the Power Pivot add-in for Excel," n.d.).

Scenario 1: Power Pivot Ribbon Disappears

1. Go to *File* > *Options* > *Add − Ins*.

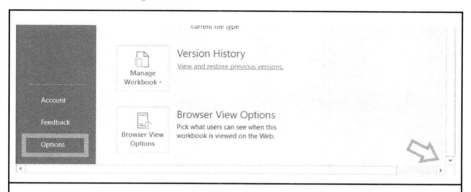

"Options" Location

Be sure to scroll down the Excel: File screen to access the File>Options screen. The Excel: File main screen was designed to be an aggregate of information, therefore, there is a lot of information here about the file and other files on your computer in some cases. This can make it difficult to find the information you need.

You will have to scroll down and navigate to the Options button to access the options window.

2. In the Manage drop-down menu, click **Disabled Items** > **Go**.

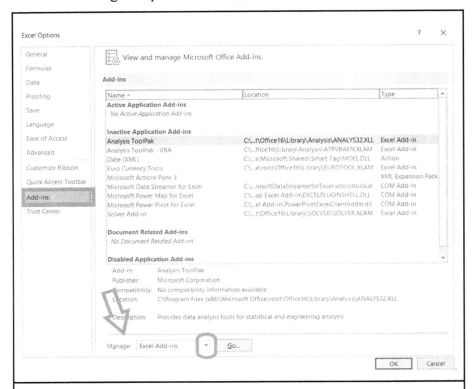

"Add-ins" Dialogue Window

Clicking "Options" will close the Excel: File window and open a separate dialogue window entitled "Excel Options". To access the Excel Options: Add-ins window, you must navigate the menu to the left. The "Manage" box is a drop-down menu at the bottom of the dialogue window. This image shows what appears in the Manage drop-down menu upon opening the window. Click the downward triangle (▼) box to navigate to **Disabled Items**.

3. Select Microsoft Office Power Pivot and then click Enable.

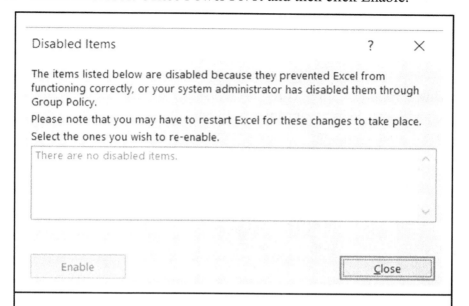

Disabled Items Dialogue Box

Clicking "OK" will prompt the Disabled Items Box. If Power Pivot was disabled it will appear in this menu. If Power Pivot isn't here, it is enabled, but it still isn't showing in the main menu, then proceed to the next scenario.

Scenario 2: Ribbon is not restored or disappears from Excel after Enabling Power Pivot

> **Note:**
>
> This solution requires edits to the system Registry. Many outfits require administrative privileges to edit the Registry, since it can affect your computer's entire operating system. You may have to get your office admin to use this solution.
>
> If you have the privileges to make the edits yourself, *take caution!* Do not make any changes to the Registry without creating a restoration point first! This can be done through ("How to Create a System Restore Point in Windows 7," n.d.):
>
> 1. *St1art > Control Panel > System and Security*
>
> 2. Click on the *System Protection* link
>
> 3. In the "System Protection" Dialogue box, click the *System Protection*tab
>
> 4. Click on *Create* button and follow the prompts

If the Power Pivot ribbon still doesn't appear, you will have to access the Registry Editor and make changes there. Follow these steps ("Start the Power Pivot add-in for Excel," n.d.):

> **Note:**
>
> Remember that the Power Pivot Add-in is only available for Windows desktop builds of Excel.

1. Close Excel and go to *Start > Run*, type in "regegit".

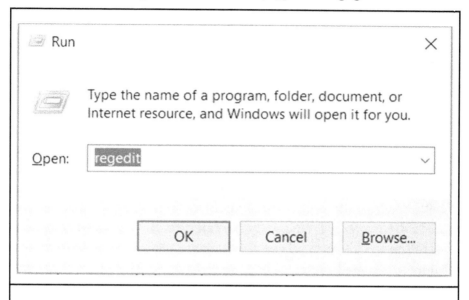

Run Dialogue Box

Going to *Start > Run* brings up the depicted small dialogue box. The Run dialogue box allows you to execute programs using their file name. This dialogue box can also be called using this keyboard shortcut: $[Windows - Key] + [R]$. Type in "regedit" and click okay to access Windows' Registry Editor.

2. Copy: $Computer\backslash HKEY\_CURRENT\_USER\backslash Software\backslash$

    $Microsoft\backslash Office\backslash [...]$

    $[...]16.0\backslash User\ Settings\backslash PowerPivotExcelAddin$ into the address bar at the top of the Registry Editor. Be sure that there are no ellipses. "[...]"

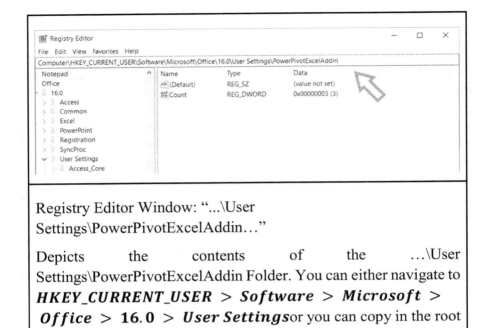

Registry Editor Window: "...\User
Settings\PowerPivotExcelAddin..."

Depicts   the   contents   of   the   ...\User
Settings\PowerPivotExcelAddin Folder. You can either navigate to
***HKEY_CURRENT_USER > Software > Microsoft >
Office > 16.0 > User Settings***or you can copy in the root
address depicted in the address bar. If you choose to copy in the
root, the Register Key is case sensitive. The root must be copied
verbatim.

3. On   the   folder   navigation   menu   on   the   left   hand   side,
   PowerPivotExcelAddin   folder   should   be   highlighted.
   Mouse: *Right − Click > Delete* the folder.

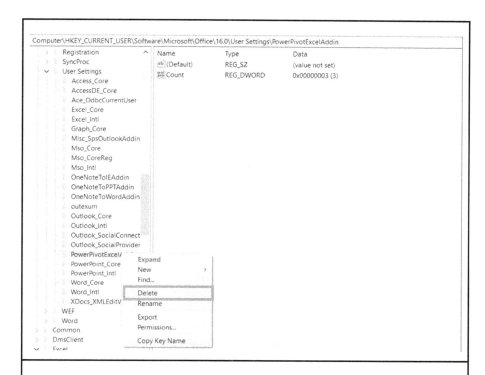

Registry   Editor   Window   Navigation: "...\User
Settings\PowerPivotExcelAddin..."

Depicts the folder navigation menu on the left-hand side of the
Registry Editor window. Whether you pasted the root or navigated
to the folder, this screenshot illustrates your target in the Registry
Editor window.

4. Copy: $Computer\HKEY_CURRENT_USER\Software\$

$Microsoft\Office\Excel\[...]$

$[...]Addins\PowerPivotExcelClientAddIn.NativeEntry.1$

into the address bar at the top of the Registry Editor. Be sure that

there are no spaces.

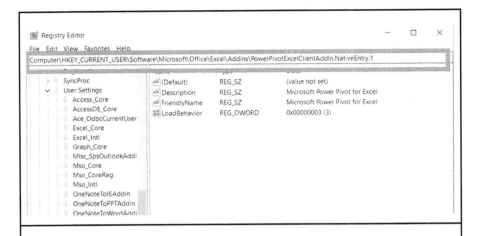

Registry Editor Window:
"...\Addins\PowerPivotExcelClientAddin..."

Depicts the contents of the
...\Addins\PowerPivotExcelClientAddin.NativeEntry.1 Folder.
You can either navigate to *HKEY_CURRENT_USER >*
Software > Microsoft > Office > Excel > Addins
or you can copy in the root address depicted in the address bar. If
you choose to copy in the root, the Register Key is case sensitive.
The root must be copied verbatim.

5. On the folder navigation menu on the left hand side, the
PowerPivotExcelClientAddIn.NativeEntry.1 folder should be
highlighted. *Mouse: Right − Click > Delete* the folder.

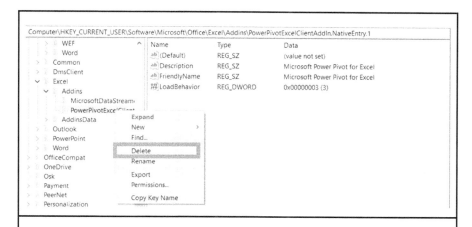

Computer\HKEY_CURRENT_USER\Software\Microsoft\Office\Excel\Addins\PowerPivotExcelClientAddIn.NativeEntry.1

Registry Editor Window Navigation: "...\Addins\PowerPivotExcelClientAddin..."

Depicts the folder navigation menu on the left-hand side of the Registry Editor window. Whether you pasted the root or navigated to the folder, this screenshot illustrates your target in the Registry Editor window.

6.   Close the Registry Editor

After completing these steps you have reset the Power Pivot Add-in on Excel. You have reinitialize as if it is a brand new install. Return to the demonstration in chapter 2 and redo the steps to gain access to the Power Pivot Add-in.

Problems with Adding Slicers

The Slicers is an Office 365 Excel 2019 feature that allows you to dynamically change the data. We covered how to deploy them in chapter about analysis in the "Creating: Discovering and validating new perspectives on the data" section. This troubleshooting section will cover problems with adding slicers.

Scenario 1: Slicer button is Inactive

Recall from chapter 1 that all modern Excel products are controlled by their licenses. For those who have a subscription service, their subscription controls what features their build of Excel will allow them to have. This same subscription based service also monitors the types of files opened on Excel. While you can open and operate an older Excel file in Office 365 Excel 2019, that file will be placed in compatibility mode to ensure the best experience. As an effect, files in compatibility mode won't have access to some features. One of those features is the advanced slicer and filter features.

To gain access to the slicer feature your file must not be in compatibility mode. Here are the steps for getting your file out of compatibility mode:

1. Go to *File* > *Info* and click on **Convert**

File>Info: Compatibility Mode

This screenshot depicts the default window that populates when you select File. This view only happens when your file is in compatibility mode. Older Excel files are placed in compatibility mode to improve performance. However, this can prevent you from using new Office 365 Excel 2019 features such as the improved slicers. Our example file was generated on an older build of Excel, therefore, it was automatically placed in compatibility mode.

2. Go back to your pivottable and you should have access to slicers.

If you still don't have slicers enabled, revisit the conditions for using slicers. For your convenience, the 4 conditions were:

1. You need to be on a desktop build of Excel

2. PivotTables need to be enabled

3. The data must be in a PivotTable

4. Must not be in compatible mode

Finally, ensure that you are engaging with a table or a pivottable. Excel spreadsheets themselves are not tables but just cells with data. Tables, and subsequently pivottables, are a recognized object within Excel.

Scenario 2: Existing Connections Dialogue Box

This dialogue box may pop up after going to *Insert > Filters > Slicer* or while you are trying to segment your pivottables.

Existing Connections Dialogue Box

Screenshot of the dialogue box that propagates when no table or pivot table is selected. This is a verbose error that is trying to communicate a lack of a target.

This error occurs when no table or pivottable is targeted. The solution is to close the window and select a pivot table or table.

Conclusion

This text follows the logical steps from getting started to finalizing a report. First and foremost, you must consider Excel versions and compatibility. This often makes the difference between a freelance data entry and consulting analyst position. Excel files are backwards compatible, meaning that newer builds of Excel will always be able to execute older Excel files. However, Microsoft uses a forwards incompatibility model, and older perpetual licenses are not able to execute newer Excel files. This is important because your client will not be able to review the delivered pivot tables embedded in an Office 365 Excel 2019 file on their old perpetual licensed build. One immediate work around is to present your build on Excel for the web, which is capable of displaying all Excel 2019 features.

This text also overviewed the new Office 365 Excel 2019 functions, which were engineered to reduce expression complexity. These conditional statements and decision based switching functions add a powerful tool for automation outside of VBA. Deploying these functions in pivottables also make the Excel for the web work around more feasible, since Excel for web does not have access to macro ("Work with VBA macros in Excel for the web," n.d.). It is also good since many corporate outfits either limit or ban the use of macro-enabled files for security. Learning how to create macros in VBA is still an excellent

"Excel power-user" skill, since it saves time in research and development outfits where macro enabled files are more tolerated. Using modular macros that handle repetitive analytical and report generating tasks is the best practice for using macros. Having one dedicated macro enabled machine for creating reports is also best practice for security in your own outfit.

We also overviewed the analysis process for large datasets, which includes investigative modeling. Of course, the approach of modeling will depend on the nature of the data, but the analysis process is universal for all projects using pivot tables:

1. Making more intelligible views of large data sets through aggregation into pivottables

2. Using modeling to investigate how the data trends and postulate why it trends with several views of the data

3. Creating new perspectives of viewing the data informed by trends and educated ascertations

Finally, we discussed best practices for reporting data and Excel features that assist with implementing these best practices. Many wizards and prompts in Excel have best practices built in, such as labeling and improved text handling using $TEXTJOIN()$ in Office 365 Excel 2019. Throughout the text, we have shared notes about Excel feature compatibility and workarounds for presenting Excel files in dated perpetual outfits. In general, data and reports can be viewed in Excel for the web. A desktop build of Excel is required to edit pivottables and reports.

Beyond specific "Power User skills," the most important aspect to take away from this text is the Power User mindset: how to use a feature to achieve some specific goal. Remember that there is a difference between features and how to use them, and the *functionality* of a feature. Excel and its pivottables are merely a tool for extracting potentially decision informing insights from large datasets.

People tend to overlook the creative aspects of data analysis, since "creativity" is usually associated with some abstract, boundless activity reserved for people in the artistic field. Even artists have to practice techniques to properly render and represent ideas that inform culture. It takes a similar methodical approach to be truly successful and insightful in research settings as well. Your presentations must answer why this dataset matters and how it will impact your client's bottom line.

Most importantly, data analysts must have integrity. We discussed scientific integrity, and models that follow the basic principles in data modeling are considered to be scientifically sound. Those that do not follow the principles can be due to human error, which is why Microsoft has wizards that mitigate this risk. However, individuals who make a deliberate choice to modify their models to support their beliefs lack professional integrity. There may be times when peers or even your superiors will ask for models that affirm their efforts in sales, outreach, or other items. It is always best to be truthful and provide an accurate reflection of the data to maintain not only your integrity, but the integrity of the data analysis field.

Reference

Bar graph missing zero1—Misleading graph—Wikipedia. (n.d.). Retrieved August 26, 2019, from https://en.wikipedia.org/wiki/Misleading_graph#/media/File:Bar_graph_missing_zero1.svg

Consolidate multiple data sources in a PivotTable. (n.d.). Retrieved August 27, 2019, from https://support.office.com/en-us/article/consolidate-multiple-data-sources-in-a-pivottable-8f476919-40b3-4133-9870-26f4d9f21ad6

Create a PivotTable to analyze worksheet data. (n.d.). Retrieved August 20, 2019, from https://support.office.com/en-us/article/create-a-pivottable-to-analyze-worksheet-data-a9a84538-bfe9-40a9-a8e9-f99134456576

File:Example truncated bar graph.svg—Wikimedia Commons. (n.d.). Retrieved August 26, 2019, from https://commons.wikimedia.org/wiki/File:Example_truncated_bar_graph.svg

File:Scatter Plot with missing categories.svg—Wikimedia Commons. (n.d.). Retrieved August 26, 2019, from https://commons.wikimedia.org/wiki/File:Scatter_Plot_with_missing_categories.svg

FORECAST.ETS.STAT function. (n.d.). Retrieved August 24, 2019, from https://support.office.com/en-us/article/forecast-ets-stat-function-60f2ae14-d0cf-465e-9736-625ccaaa60b4

Forecasting functions (reference). (n.d.). Retrieved August 24, 2019, from https://support.office.com/en-us/article/forecasting-functions-reference-897a2fe9-6595-4680-a0b0-93e0308d5f6e

How to Create a System Restore Point in Windows 7. (n.d.). Retrieved August 23, 2019, from Dummies website: https://www.dummies.com/computers/operating-systems/windows-7/how-to-create-a-system-restore-point-in-windows-7/

IFS function. (n.d.). Retrieved August 27, 2019, from https://support.office.com/en-us/article/ifs-function-36329a26-37b2-467c-972b-4a39bd951d45

Introductory Econometrics Chapter 3: Pivot Tables. (n.d.). Retrieved August 23, 2019, from http://www3.wabash.edu/econometrics/EconometricsBook/chap3.htm

Keyboard shortcuts in Excel. (n.d.). Retrieved August 27, 2019, from https://support.office.com/en-us/article/keyboard-shortcuts-in-excel-1798d9d5-842a-42b8-9c99-9b7213f0040f

Koble, M. (n.d.). What Is the Life Span of the Average PC? | Chron.com. Retrieved August 20, 2019, from https://smallbusiness.chron.com/life-span-average-pc-69823.html

Microsoft wants you to beta test upcoming Office products and
services | Windows Central. (n.d.). Retrieved August 27, 2019,
from https://www.windowscentral.com/microsoft-wants-you-
beta-test-upcoming-office-products-and-services

Power Pivot keyboard shortcuts and accessibility—Office Support.
(n.d.). Retrieved August 26, 2019, from
https://support.office.com/en-us/article/Power-Pivot-keyboard-
shortcuts-and-accessibility-C87D45F9-FFB3-4BA9-AEB0-
687627A2B9FF

Start the Power Pivot add-in for Excel. (n.d.). Retrieved August 23,
2019, from https://support.office.com/en-us/article/start-the-
power-pivot-add-in-for-excel-a891a66d-36e3-43fc-81e8-
fc4798f39ea8

SWITCH function. (n.d.). Retrieved August 27, 2019, from
https://support.office.com/en-us/article/switch-function-
47ab33c0-28ce-4530-8a45-d532ec4aa25e

The VBA Guide To Excel Pivot Tables. (n.d.). Retrieved August 20,
2019, from The Spreadsheet Guru website:
https://www.thespreadsheetguru.com/blog/2014/9/27/vba-
guide-excel-pivot-tables

Use slicers to filter data—Office Support. (n.d.). Retrieved August 26,
2019, from https://support.office.com/en-us/article/use-slicers-
to-filter-data-249f966b-a9d5-4b0f-b31a-12651785d29d

Where is Power Pivot? (n.d.). Retrieved August 23, 2019, from
https://support.office.com/en-us/article/where-is-power-pivot-
aa64e217-4b6e-410b-8337-20b87e1c2a4b

Work with VBA macros in Excel for the web. (n.d.). Retrieved August
23, 2019, from https://support.office.com/en-gb/article/work-
with-vba-macros-in-excel-for-the-web-98784ad0-898c-43aa-
a1da-4f0fb5014343

XlConsolidationFunction enumeration (Excel) | Microsoft Docs. (n.d.).
Retrieved August 26, 2019, from
https://docs.microsoft.com/en-
us/office/vba/api/excel.xlconsolidationfunction